From

SALLY LUNNS
to CIDER SAUCE

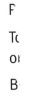

F
Tc
o
B

From
SALLY LUNNS
to CIDER SAUCE

Recipes and Memories of Somerset

Catherine Rothwell

AMBERLEY

*To my cream of a sister
from her skin and blister,
with love.*

First published 2011

Amberley Publishing
The Hill, Stroud
Gloucestershire, GL5 4EP

www.amberleybooks.com

British Library Cataloguing in Publication Data.
A catalogue record for this book is available from the British Library.

ISBN 978-1-4456-0334-6

Typesetting and Origination by Amberley Publishing.
Printed in Great Britain.

Contents

Acknowledgements

I would like to thank the following people and organisations for their assistance in the writing of this book: Barbara Strachan, Ron Severs, J. Salmon Ltd, Clovelly Village Centre, Exmoor National Park Information Centre, The National Trust, Robin Weir, Watchet Museum, Ben Norman, Mr Vowles, Somerset Magazine, Max Ley, Minehead Library, Somerset County Library, Harry Williamson, Stephen Edge, Catherine Payne, Lancashire Library Services (especially Poulton-le-Fylde Library), David Skipp, Jocelyn Houghton.

Images on the following pages are courtesy of Wikimedia Commons: 89 (4028mdk09), 99, 100 (Marcin Floryan), 101 (Lestat), 104 (Tony Wills), 105 (Frank C. Miller), 110 (Aka), 113 (Stu Spivack) and 116 (Wurzeller).

Loyal readers of mine may notice that I have reproduced some recipes from previous books. Since these works are now out of print, and for the sake of having the best of Somerset in a single volume, I thought it would be worth repeating myself, just this once.

Author's Note

Most of the recipes in this book are designed to serve a family of five. Where there are exceptions, I have mentioned it in the text. All spoon measures are level. Recipes using lighly cooked eggs should be avoided by infants, the elderly, convalescents, pregnant women and anyone suffering from an illness. Vegetables and fruit should be well washed. The times given are approximate.

Conversion Guides

Oven Temperatures

	°C	°F	Gas Mark
Very Cool	110	225	¼
	120	250	½
Cool	140	275	1
	150	300	2
Moderate	160	325	3
	180	350	4
Moderately Hot	190	375	5
	200	400	6
Hot	220	425	7
	230	450	8
Very Hot	240	475	9

Oven temperatures and cooking times are intended as a guide. If you are using a fan oven, reduce temperatures by 20 °F.

Imperial Weights and Measures
(with Recommended Metric Equivalents)

Ounces	Grams	Ounces	Grams
1	25	9	250
2	50	10	275
3	75	11	300
4	110	12	350
5	50	13	375
6	175	14	400
7	200	15	425
8	225	16	450

Pints	Fluid Ounces	Millilitres
¼	5	150
½	10	300
¾	15	450
1	20	600
1½	30	900
1¾	35	1,000

1 cup flour = 4 oz = 110 g
1 cup sugar = 6 oz = 175 g
1 cup butter = 8 oz = 225 g

Introduction

Searching for detailed information about transport, habits and places from the past, I have examined hundreds of old photographs and picture postcards in the years since I retired. Minehead must emerge as one of the top ten holiday destinations, if the sending of postcards while on holiday is anything to go by. The card that says it all is of St Michael's church. How well I remember the sight of crimson fuchsia against white cottage walls, and the most luxuriant of lavender, easily vying the Mediterranean's.

By the 1880s, the English had developed an enormous appetite for cheap day trips. One works outing from an industrial area in September 1844 involved 'a train of 240 carriages drawn by 9 engines, carrying 6,600 passengers' according to an 1844 report in the *Fleetwood Chronicle*. Each had paid two shillings for a third-class return ticket to the seaside. It was enough in those days to sniff the sea breezes (ozone, they called it), feel the sands under your boots, and sample shrimps with tea and buns. A holiday like that was perhaps the sole outing of any distance in a whole year, and it was only made possible by the new-fangled railways.

In the West Country in 1895, *Tantivy*, the well-appointed, fast, four-horse coach of Messrs Jones Brothers that carried the mails, ran daily throughout the year, Sundays excepted, in connection with the trains of the London & South Western Railway. In the summer season there were two additional coaches, *Tally Ho* and *Glen Lyn*, which set the countryside ringing with their coach horns or 'yards of tin'.

A century before this, such famous artists and poets as Turner, Coleridge, Shelley, Wordsworth and Southey – each having heard travellers' tales – sought out the district. They were a select group, but they were spearheading the many thousands who were to follow.

Thirty years ago I came with my family for the first time to the county of combes and stayed at beautiful Halsway Manor, which I believe is now used for educational courses. We walked in the Quantocks and Brendon Hills and visited Crowcombe, Stogumber, Dunster, Minehead, Dunkery, Cothelstone Beacon, Bagborough, Blue Anchor, Weston (the only place in Britain where the wild peony grows), East and West Quantoxhead and Watchet, which was a flourishing port in the days of the Danes (here we looked for fossils and explored rock pools). There were also visits to the Yellow Pottery, days watching the huntsmen and pack, and rides on the train. We loved it all.

As a historian and collector of old country recipes, I found Somerset a happy hunting ground, seemingly never to be exhausted. Old recipes tied in with tradition and history, for example the dish that is eaten on Plough Monday, the Monday following the Feast of Epiphany, when the village plough was taken into church and blessed. Collops of beef are prepared on Collop Monday. Stinging nettle soup is an old country remedy for anaemia, nettles being one of the best sources of minerals. Fennel aids digestion and is good for relieving babies' colic. Neatsfoot oil eases the aches and pains of agricultural labourers. 'To soothe a burned mouth, chew a clean comfrey leaf,' I was told, and there were other stories recounted, like the one of the feast on Lady Day, when rents were paid. It was customary to bury a side of venison in readiness for the feast. A side retrieved from a dubious spot was once voted by unsuspecting farmers 'the best venison ever'.

Watchet, the 1,000-year-old port, had a court leet that survived into the 1980s. Among its ancient duties was the appointment of port reeve, ale taster and pig drover. After swearing in, 'all sat down to a hearty meal of roast goose followed by hot punch and walnuts' according to a newspaper report of the day. The port reeve's account for 'vitals on 26 October 1746' lists, 'for a rump of beef 3/4d; a surloyne of beef 4/4d; a leg of mutton 2/-; for candell light 1/6d ...'

Somerset and district retain their fascination and unspoiled beauty. In this book I have tried to 'call back yesterday, bid time return', so that once again memories from times past, of cob and thatch, of cliffs and combes and windy heights, can be savoured.

Memories of Somerset surface – swarms of tortoiseshell butterflies encircling purple buddleia like satellites, and the huge stag suddenly appearing on the moorland bracken, pausing, head thrown back, antlers stark against the skyline. Moments later, the red coat of the leading huntsman flashed forth, the thin note of his pursuing horn echoing for what seemed miles.

We had wonderful walks in the Quantocks and around Dunkery Beacon, where on clear days there is a view of four counties. In the early mornings, mysterious swathes of vapour clothed the countryside, draping ancient, thick hedgerows alive with multiple species. Quantoxhead, Stogumber and Bishops Lydeard are names instantly recalled. Unforgettable, too, were trips to Blue Anchor bay with its rock pools, red cliffs and ammonites. Here, we once saw a perfect rainbow springing from the Quantocks and arcing the bay. Wells, Glastonbury, Bath, Cheddar, the Mendips and the Somerset Levels were reserved for further visits, and collectively we came to view Somerset as a land of promise, a county of rich diversity. Every visit added to this conviction; each was a golden opportunity to collect recipes.

Somerset cooking, we found, is best expressed as hearty meat dishes, 'staying puddings', casseroles, stews and delicious pies. All rely heavily on local ingredients, which are exploited to the full. Cider, cream, fish, apples, venison and lamb are the mainstays. The South Downs lamb gains subtle flavour from grazing on thymey uplands. Lamb raised on Exmoor and fattened on the farming areas at its foot also gains superb flavour. This is also true of the trout found in the rivers that are fed by the peaty streams flowing from Exmoor.

I sincerely hope that sampling these recipes will prove as enjoyable as their collection. As time went by, I began to strongly suspect that the famous people in the past who discovered Somerset – Wordsworth, Coleridge, Turner and others – stayed on for the food, and who could blame them?

The Main Meal

Roast Lamb

METHOD
Peel and slice the potatoes. Into a roasting tin put the sliced potatoes and onions. Put in the stock. Place the lamb on top, scatter it with the rosemary, and put it into a hot oven. Cook for 2 hours, lowering the oven temperature towards the end of cooking, by which time some evaporation has allowed the potato tops to brown and the meat juices to flavour the vegetables. It is best to trim any surplus fat from the joint before cooking.

INGREDIENTS

a shoulder of lamb
3 small onions, sliced
1 lb potatoes
seasoning
1 pint lamb stock
1 teaspoon chopped
rosemary

EXFORD

When, in 1857, the old church of St Audrey at Quantoxhead was to be rebuilt, its beautiful fifteenth-century fan-vaulted rood screen was 'rudely' stacked in an old barn, where it lay for forty years until its value was recognised. Because it fitted perfectly, it came to Exford church. Exford was the centre for the Devon and Somerset stag hunt. There is still a forge there, and sheep auctions are held three times a year. The River Exe is a glorious sight after heavy rains.

Lamb and Rosemary

METHOD

Preheat an oven to 450 °F. With some of the butter, grease a baking dish to suit the size of the lamb portion. Put in the rosemary and bay leaf, sprinkling well with salt and pepper. Pour the stock into the pan and spread the lamb with the rest of the butter. Cover with buttered paper and bake for three-quarters of an hour, then remove the paper and brown the meat. The skimmed gravy can then be strained over the meat.

INGREDIENTS

2 lb breast of lamb
a sprig of rosemary
1 bay leaf
salt and pepper
2 oz fresh butter
4 pints stock

MINEHEAD

Before the Norman Conquest, Minehead belonged to Algar, Earl of Mercia, who was not only Lord of the Manor of Porlock but a son of Lady Godiva. William de Mohun, who had helped William the Conqueror at the Battle of Hastings, was rewarded with Minehead and Dunster Castle. Queen Elizabeth made Minehead a borough and up to 1832, when the franchise was reformed, two MPs represented its interests. Local men of note include Sir Thomas Dyke Acland, Allan Hughes and Colonel N. W. Wiggans, master of the Devon and Somerset Staghounds, who in 1935 presented thousands of acres of moorland bordering Minehead for the use of the nation. Minehead Gardens, as shown in the postcard from the 1930s, was created from land near the sea.

Braised Lamb

*A sixteenth-century 'Serving Man's Song' praises all
meat above wealth: 'Oh for a plump, fat leg of mutton/
Veal, lamb, capon, pig and coney/None is happy but a
glutton/None an ass but who wants money.'*

INGREDIENTS

2 lb loin of lamb
a lemon
1 oz butter
a large Spanish onion
a blade of mace
1 dessertspoon mixed
   rosemary and thyme
1 gill cream
1 teaspoon arrowroot
2 rashers bacon
½ pint of water
a dish of your favourite
   forcemeat

METHOD
Bone the lamb and skin downwards. Cover with
forcemeat, roll up and secure with butcher's
skewers. Put the bones in a saucepan with the
peeled, chopped onion, the thyme and rosemary
and two slices of lemon, peeled and pithless. Add
water. Rub the lamb with a piece of cut lemon
and spread the rashers of bacon on it. Place the
lamb on the bones in the pan, cover well and cook
gently for 2 hours.

Take out the lamb and keep it hot. Strain the
liquid into a bowl and after skimming; boil it
quickly to reduce in volume. Mix the arrowroot
with a little cold water, stir it into the pan, and
continue stirring until it has boiled for 5 minutes. Put in the butter and
cream but do not allow to boil. This rich sauce is poured over the lamb. Vegetables are
placed around the joint to serve as a garnish. Serve with forcemeat in a separate dish.
Suitable recipes can be found on pages 22 and 32.

MINEHEAD: GOVERNMENT AND MEDIA

In the 1930s, with a population of about 8,000, Minehead was governed by an
Urban District Council of sixteen members. The town's seal, showing a ship over a
woolpack, is a symbol of Minehead's early commerce. Local newspapers were the
West Somerset Free Press, County Gazette and *Express and Echo.* The postcard of old
cottages and Quay Town under North Hill was sent on 15 August 1953 by 'Ethel
and Harry': 'Having a lovely
holiday in the car … staying on
the sea front.' After doing most
of the favoured trips – Clovelly,
Dunkery, Weston, Bath – the
holidaymakers were enjoying
the gardens and beach prior to
motoring on to the Wye Valley.

Boiled Lamb in Caper Sauce

This is a very old lamb recipe in Somerset. In the seventeenth and eighteenth centuries, meat was often boiled this way. Perhaps, for some, it was the only way.

METHOD
Place the lamb in a large pan and cover with the water, spices and salt. Bring slowly to the boil, skim, then slowly simmer, allowing 20 minutes to the pound. Then simmer for another 20 minutes. A ham joint or an old chicken could be done in the same way.

To make the caper sauce, use the water in which you have cooked the meat (a quarter to half a pint). Melt the lard or dripping and slowly blend in the flour. Mix it well, then put in the capers and cook on for about 8 minutes. This gives a delicate flavour to the lamb. To boil for too long at this point results in too strong a flavour. In the eighteenth century an oyster and anchovy sauce was used on old fowl.

INGREDIENTS

1 leg of lamb
1 teaspoon salt
½ teaspoon allspice

For the sauce:
1 oz lard or dripping
10 oz flour
¼ pint of milk
2 tablespoons of pickled capers

MINEHEAD: GHOSTS AND BATHING

Visitors in the 1920s were told by a popular 1920 holiday guide, 'The bathing in Minehead is safe, the best time being from two hours before to two hours after high water. Bathing outside the limits of Minehead Bay is risky.' There were huts for hire along the beach; before that, there were bathing machines. On the front, floodlit at night, a sea-water swimming bath with showers and a sun-bathing area was available from the early 1930s, which was when this photograph is of Minehead Sands and North Hill was taken.

One legend attached to Minehead is of the whistling ghost, which used to go by the shore or frequent the quay. Its whistling, even on a calm day, would cause a severe storm to blow up and wreck ships. In the seventeenth century, the Bishop of Bath and Wells was beseeched to exorcise the pest.

South Country Pie

METHOD
Wash and stone the plums and place them in a pie
dish, sprinkled with spice and sugar. Add a layer of
chops and onions. Seasoning as you go, continue
layering until the ingredients are all used. Squeeze
the lemon juice over the top. Place a pastry crust
upon the dish and bake in a moderate oven for 1½
hours. The pastry may have originally been suet.
Rub in the flour and margarine and bind with a
little water. It is necessary to cover the crust with
two sheets of parchment paper, wrung out in water,
to prevent over-browning.

INGREDIENTS

1 lb sour plums
2 lb lamb chops
2 teaspoons sugar
2 onions
1 lemon
a little brown sugar and
spice

For the pastry:
8 oz flour
3 oz low-cholesterol
margarine

Mutton Casserole

This eighteenth-century recipe uses anchovies and herbs. Some elderly people today are enthusiastic about the flavour of mutton, but it does not seem to be readily available, so lamb could be used instead.

METHOD
Roll the cubed meat in seasoned flour and fry until browned, to seal. Also fry the chopped vegetables in the lard. Add the flour to make a roux (see page 116). Stir well, but be gentle in order to not splash fat. Continue as you slowly add the stock, which is best made from a good-quality vegetable cube. Scatter on the herbs, then bring to the boil as the roux thickens. Put all in a lidded casserole dish. Cook in the oven at 400 °F for 2 hours. If you have used mutton, cook for 3 hours for tenderness.

INGREDIENTS

2 oz lard
1 lb cubed stewing lamb
2 oz seasoned flour
1 pint stock
1 lb chopped onions
1 lb chopped carrots and turnips
½ teaspoon mixed herbs
2 oz flour

LEISURE IN MINEHEAD

This photograph of the Esplanade dates from August 1936. Asphalted and protected by a sea wall, it commands a fine view of the bay, with its splendid sands and safe bathing. In Jubilee Gardens, where an orchestra played, a café catered for visitors. Minehead is sheltered by hills, the most prominent being North Hill, overlooking the ancient harbour hundreds of feet below. A profusion of flowers and shrubs in the open air, blooming well into autumn, is proof of the mildness of the climate and the sheltered position. The floodlit terraces of the swimming pool designed for 500 bathers could accommodate 2,000 spectators, who would arrive for weekly exhibitions.

Country Farm Sausages, or Hog's Pudding

Some of the best recipes for this traditional dish have been handed down over generations by Somerset pork butchers and are well guarded secrets. Here is one of them.

METHOD
Soak some pig skins in salted water. Mix together the minced pork, breadcrumbs and mixed herbs. Season thoroughly with salt and pepper. Fill the skins with this mixture and tie the ends of each tightly. Boil till cooked.

Hog's Pudding is delicious sliced and eaten cold, fried with bacon, bread or egg, or even put into a pasty.

INGREDIENTS

some pig skins
1 pint salted water
2 lb minced pork
8 oz breadcrumbs
½ teaspoon sage
½ teaspoon thyme
½ marjoram
salt and pepper

THE ORIGINAL RECIPES

Several recipes in this book came into my possession thirty years ago, when I was given a little black notebook owned by a Weston housewife in the 1890s. It is now falling to pieces, but her handwriting is still legible, and the recipes have stood the test of time. The recipes on the right are for sausage, pork pies and mincemeat.

Sausage Forcemeat

METHOD
Mix the
sausage meat
with the other
ingredients
thoroughly,
then moisten
with the stock.

INGREDIENTS

½ lb pork sausage meat
½ teaspoon chopped fresh
herbs
a small quantity of grated
lemon rind
1 tablespoon breadcrumbs
1 tablespoon stock

WRINGTON

This building at Barley Wood, Wrington, is interesting as being one of the houses
that belonged to Hannah More, a pioneer in education, especially among the
children in the Mendip area. She died in 1833, having lived also at Cowslip Green,
not far from Barley Wood. Hannah wrote a series of easy-to-read booklets
and attracted grown-ups and children to Sunday schools, such as in Cheddar.
Soon, over a million children were being educated at Sunday schools all over
the country. Wrington was part of the vast estates of Glastonbury, but passed
to Sir Henry Capel in 1546. His descendants were staunch Royalists. The great
philosopher John Locke was born close to Wrington church in 1632. Altered and
added to over many years, the chancel dates back to the early fourteenth century.

Baked Ham in Cider

METHOD

Omitting any seasoning, I did not find it necessary to soak the ham overnight. Jim Watson, master butcher, agreed that in doing so, some flavour would be lost. The ham, however, has to be a prime piece. Put in a large pan with cider, onion, nutmeg and lemon. Simmer for half an hour. Mix the breadcrumbs and sugar. Take out the ham, let it cool and press the crumbs and sugar (bound with a little water) all over the ham.

INGREDIENTS

4 lb joint lean gammon
1 pint cider
1 Spanish onion
sprigs of parsley
2 tablespoons brown sugar
3 tablespoons breadcrumbs
a pinch of nutmeg
½ lemon

At this point put the ham in an oven-proof dish to which has been added just less than half a pint of stock from the pan. Bake in a hot oven for 40 minutes and the top will crisp. Larger joints will need longer. Damson pickle is the favoured Somerset dressing with baked ham. Use parsley as a garnish.

SIDBURY MANOR

The manor held its court leet on the third Wednesday in November. It elected manorial officers whose responsibilities in medieval times included ale-tasting, bread-weighing and meat-tasting, thereby ensuring that villagers had good milk, ale, bread and meat.

Casserole of Pork from Taunton

METHOD
Simmer the meat with the peppercorns and bay
leaves for an hour. In the melted pork dripping,
gently brown the onion and apple. Place these in
a heat-proof casserole dish and add the prepared
vegetables. Add the piece of pork, followed by the
cider, stock and raisins. Cook in a moderate oven for
2 hours.

INGREDIENTS

3 lb joint of pork with
skin removed
6 peppercorns
2 sliced, peeled and cored
apples
4 bay leaves
2 sliced leeks (white part
only)
1 large, sliced Spanish
onion
¼ pint stock made from
chicken bones
3 oz seedless raisins
1 oz pork dripping
½ pint cider

TAUNTON

A visitor from Minehead in the days of this
photograph could reach Taunton by wagonette,
motor charabanc or rail. Today's journey along
the preserved West Somerset Railway takes
one past extremely beautiful scenery and is
very popular. Taunton's spacious streets belie
its long history, which began in Saxon days.
Perkin Warbeck seized the town in 1497, but it was later
captured by Henry VII. The Civil War saw much bloodshed, and Judge Jeffreys
and Colonel Kirke's cruel prosecutions – meted out at the Bloody Assizes held
at Taunton Castle in 1685 – are an indelible part of Somerset's past. The brutality
with which Judge Jeffreys meted out punishment – 200 were hanged and 800
transported – has led to stories of his haunting the West Country. Taunton Castle
still echoes to the tramp of soldiers and prisoners. Spirits hang as balls of light
and phantom horsemen flee down the Sedgemoor lanes. Now used as a museum,
the great hall (where the
hanging sentences were
read out) still stands. A
twelfth-century priory
barn, a row of thatched
almshouses, an ancient
packhorse bridge and
the White Hart Inn
– the old coaching house
where Colonel Kirke
stayed after Monmouth's
rebellion – are also still
in existence.

Celery Cream

METHOD

Remove the outer leaves from the celery and cut off the green tops. Wash the white celery thoroughly and cut into short lengths. Place these in boiling water and cook for 8 minutes. Drain. Lay the celery in cold water. Cut up the bacon finely and put in a cast-iron casserole dish. Add the onion and carrot, peeled and sliced into rings. Drain the cold water from the celery and put it in the casserole dish. Cover with the milk and simmer until the celery is cooked through. Drain off the liquid and boil it down to ½ pint. Then slowly add the cream and seasoning. Pour this sauce over the celery and serve.

INGREDIENTS

1 good stick of autumn celery
2 rashers fatty bacon
1 large onion
1 carrot
2 tbsp cream
1 pint skimmed milk
ground sea salt and pepper

Nineteenth-Century Casserole of Rabbit

METHOD

Wash and joint a rabbit. Half-fill the casserole with water and place the joints of rabbit inside. Add a nut of butter and a good sprinkle of pepper. Put salt and rings of onion on top. Cook the covered casserole of rabbit for 1½ hours in a moderate oven.

INGREDIENTS

1 rabbit
½ cup fresh breadcrumbs
1 teaspoon rubbed sage
1 tablespoon butter
salt and pepper
1 large onion thinly sliced into rings

QUAY STREET, MINEHEAD

A view of Quay Street in the 1920s, with the Red Lion Hotel (offering 'Hancock's Flagon Ales and Stouts') on the left. A gentleman on a tricycle rides up Quay Street, which is otherwise devoid of traffic. In those days, Minehead was a quiet place in which to write a novel – I. E. Patterson's *Love Like the Sea*, Helen P. Lewis's *Rudder and the Rock* and E. N. Bungey's *The Fordington Twins* were all set in Minehead. Many historical novels were written about the Quantock Hills and the famous novelist Thomas Hardy used Dunster as the setting for *A Laodicean*. Porlock featured in Marie Corelli's *The Treasure of Heaven*. Many famous people, including artists, geologists, poets and naturalists, have visited and written about this lovely part of the world.

Rabbit and Onion Bake

Pork could be substituted for rabbit. The importance of the pig and its widespread use in old recipes is instanced by mention in a seventeenth-century will, which included among the bequests, 'one quarter of the hogg now a'fatting in the yard, when he is killed'.

INGREDIENTS

a jointed rabbit
4 oz stale bread, crumbled
salt and pepper
mixed herbs
3 rashers bacon
½ lb parboiled onions

METHOD

Arrange the rabbit in a baking tin, mixing with it the bread. Season all with pepper, salt and mixed herbs. Arrange the bacon over this and, when they are ready, the onions. Pour the onion water gently over the rabbit. Bake in a moderate oven for 1½ hours, basting at frequent intervals.

NORTH WALK, MINEHEAD

This popular postcard by A. R. Quinton was sent from Minehead in the 1920s and shows the North Walk, a coastal stretch recommended for invalids who needed fresh air. It is possible that Ellen Gregory, the wife of George Stephenson, walked or was pushed in a bath chair here, for she died at Minehead in 1865. Iron bath chairs were made for use in hot climates; in 1884 you could buy one for two guineas. In the same year, ladies were wearing Swanbill corsets, Egerton Burnett's serges, and the renowned Louis Velveteen cloth, which was made into long, close-fitting gowns. Invalids were advised to wear uncomfortable-looking 'electropathic' belts. Long ago Minehead was called Munheved, which was possibly derived from the Saxon word 'heved' or, alternatively, the town's connection with William de Mohun.

Potted Hough

I discovered that a hough was a hock, or a leg of beef. This recipe originated in Scotland, but has long been popular in Somerset.

INGREDIENTS

3 lb hough
salt and pepper

METHOD

Place in a saucepan a 3 lb hough which the butcher has broken well and cover entirely with water. Put it on the fire at night, let it nearly boil. Then place it on the hob and let it simmer gently all night, not boil. In the morning, the meat will fall from the bones. Mince the meat. Remove the bones and put meat back into pan. Add a little boiling water, pepper and salt to taste, and after 10 minutes only, pot in dishes or bowls and put it aside to cool and set.

Ox Cheek

METHOD

Boil ox head for 2 hours. Take the meat off the bones and lay the pieces in a mould. Press down. Strain the liquor in which the head was boiled. Season with pepper and salt and a spoon of ketchup if you so desire. Place the mould in the oven and bake for an hour, having moistened the meat in the mould with the liquor. What is left of this can later be reduced in content, thickened with a little flour, and served with the mould.

INGREDIENTS

4 lb head of ox
salt and pepper
tomato ketchup

MINEHEAD AND THE IRISH

'Arrived at Minehead last night before a storm lasting 3 hours. We left Weston, coming through Cheddar, Wells, Glastonbury, Taunton and Blue Anchor Bay.' This was written in 1929, apparently from the Hopcott Hotel, Minehead. Centuries before, geographer Leland argued that 'the fairest part of the town standeth in the bottom of an hill'. When he came to Minehead it was 'exceedingly full of Irish menne'. Ireland sent cattle and wool to the port and Minehead became prosperous on this trade; the beautiful parish church of St Michael reflects the wealth of the town's merchants. The opening of Butlin's Holiday Camp in 1962 meant a large influx of another kind of visitor.

Eighteenth-Century Venison Pasty

METHOD

Cover the meat with the seasoned flour. Melt the butter in a pan and brown the meat to seal it. Add the lemon juice, herbs, seasoning and enough stock and red wine to cover the meat. Bring to the boil then simmer gently for 1½ hours. Place in a large pie dish and cover with a thick, flaky pastry lid brushed with beaten egg (see page 88). Cook for 30 minutes at 350 °F until the pastry is browned.

INGREDIENTS

2 lbs shoulder or breast of
    venison (cut up)
a bunch of fresh herbs
ground sea salt and
    pepper
8 oz flaky pastry
2 oz butter
2 oz seasoned flour
juice of 1 lemon
1 pint stock
a little red wine
1 beaten egg

MINEHEAD: FROM HARBOUR TO RESORT

Minehead's harbour was once regarded as, next to that of Bristol, the safest on the channel. Trade was considerable and it was important for its fisheries, but commerce diminished because of competition from other ports. The Minehead herring was famous, but by the 1920s, as at other places, the once-plentiful shoals had disappeared. The town then blossomed as a health resort, thanks to its mild climate and sheltered situation. From the 1850s onwards, its proximity to Exmoor and the revival in the hunting of Red Deer brought it into notice again. As frost and snow are rare, invalids sought out Minehead for regular holidays or for convalescence.

This beautiful study was taken in the early 1930s and the message on the back reads, 'I like Minehead – it reminds me of Southport all lit by fairy lamps.'

Venison with Sauce

Venison was served hundreds of years ago in halls and medieval castles when those 'below the salt', i.e. the peasantry, were served 'umbles', the entrails of deer, and so 'ate umble pie'. Those 'above the salt' received the choicest roast venison.

INGREDIENTS

2 lb venison
¼ lb lard

For the sauce:
½ pint red wine
1 onion
1 tablespoon flour
3 teaspoons mashed anchovy
1 teaspoon thyme

METHOD

Rub the joint of venison well with lard, cover with foil and roast at 350 °F, 35 minutes to the pound. Allow to brown, towards the end, by removing the foil.

To make the sauce, collect the juices from the roast venison and add the chopped onion. Stir in flour, wine, anchovy and thyme. Cook, stirring all the time until it thickens. Serve with the venison.

HUNTING

Ideas on hunting have changed in the century or so since this postcard, 'Landing the deer, Porlock Weir', was sent in August 1908. The dogs are the Devon and Somerset Staghounds, a alternative pack being the Quantock and Tiverton Staghounds. The stag-hunting season

began at the end of July and finished mid-October. From then until March, hind-hunting was permitted. Dulverton, Dunster, Porlock, Lynton and Minehead were considered the best centres: 'Good mounts are obtainable ... the runs with Devon and Somerset are unequalled for pace, length and excitement,' said a 1902 tourist guide. Two guineas a day for fox- and hind-hunting and 4½ guineas a day for stag-hunting was charged; the hacking charge was 7s 6d a day. Two fox-hunting packs ranged Exmoor and east of Minehead, including the Quantocks. The West Somerset Foxhounds hunted the county between Minehead and Bridgwater in two packs. The kennels for one pack were sited at Carhampton, near Minehead. An average of 100 foxes were killed each season.

Stuffed Roast Chicken

METHOD

Flavour was added by inserting chopped parsley under the chicken skin before cooking. The herbs were mixed with soft butter to form an easily spread paste. Chopped thyme and lemon thyme could also be added to the chopped parsley.

INGREDIENTS

1 chicken

For the stuffing:
4 oz sausage meat
2 chopped, peeled apples
1 tablespoon breadcrumbs
1 tablespoon chopped parsley

Mix all the ingredients for the stuffing together. As of old, the recipe recommends placing the stuffing in the bird. I cooked this separately, in a buttered loaf tin, for three quarters of an hour at the same oven temperature as the chicken and served it all together. Rather than stuff the bird, grandmother used to put half a lemon with a faggot of herbs inside the cavity.

Put the bird into a roasting tin, cover loosely with greaseproof paper, and roast in a hot oven at 400 °F, lowering the temperature for the last hour of cooking. Remove the paper, baste and allow the chicken to brown in the last 20 minutes.

CROWCOMBE

Our favourite of the villages in the Quantock Hills is notable for its cob cottages, built from a mixture of mud and straw. The best approach on a good day out, we found, was over the Quantocks from Nether Stowey.

In 1725, the top of the church spire there was struck by lightning and crashed down into the churchyard, where it still remains. The terrified worshippers huddled in the church porch, unharmed. A worn market cross reminds visitors of an annual fair that began in 1234. It is no longer held, but on the worn step of the village cross much butter, cheese and poultry must have once changed hands.

Tenderising an Old Bird

METHOD

Clean bird, reserving giblets. Remove lumps of
chicken fat. Sprinkle with seasoning. Cover the
giblets with cold water, season, and bring to boil for
three-quarters of an hour. Chop the chicken liver
finely and mix with all the stuffing ingredients.
Stuff the bird. Brown the chicken in heated oil and
put into a large dish. Add chopped onions, leeks
and apples. Season, then pour the giblet stock and
the wine over the bird. Cook in a moderate oven,
350 °F for 1½ hours.

The potatoes should be peeled, sliced, rolled in
seasoned flour and added to the casserole about
one hour before the end of cooking time.

INGREDIENTS

a large chicken
4 medium sized sliced
onions
2 chopped baby leeks
2 chopped green apples
salt and pepper
3 oz seasoned flour
½ pint dry white wine
1 lb potatoes
2 tablespoons corn oil

For the stuffing:
4 oz sausage meat
2 chopped cooking apples
1 tablespoon breadcrumbs
1 tablespoon fresh
chopped parsley
1 teaspoon thyme

MINEHEAD'S CHURCHES

Near the foot of North Hill is the old parish
church, which also served as lighthouse long
years ago.

To aid mariners, a light was kept
burning in the tower. This postcard, sent
in August 1939, shows St. Michael's church
above the cobbled, stepped street running
between old thatched cottages.

In front of St Andrew's church in the town
of Minehead was placed the canopied statue
of Queen Anne by Francis Bird. Once, it was
sited within the church. It is referred to in the
churchwardens' accounts: 'Ringing when the
Queen's effigies was brought to Church 7/6d.'
'Paid for beer for the men that brought it into
Church 2/6d.'

At low water in Minehead Bay, traces of
a subterranean forest are still evident. Flints
from prehistoric times have been found there.

Chicken in Cider

METHOD
Place the chicken in an oven-proof dish with a scattering of chopped sage on the breast. Add the chopped onions and apples. Add seasoning. Pour over the cider and the white stock. Cook all in a hot oven for 1½ hours.

INGREDIENTS

1 chicken, about 3 lb in weight
4 medium sliced onions
2 chopped baking apples
1 tablespoon chopped sage
½ pint cider
½ pint white stock
seasoning

Chicken in Aspic

METHOD
Slice eggs and place in the bottom of a tin mould. Add cooked peas then chicken in small pieces. Put water and gelatine in a pan and melt over low heat. Make the stock from a chicken stock cube and sieve into the gelatine. Cover mixture in mould with this liquid and when cool, chill in the fridge. Serve sliced with a fresh green salad.

INGREDIENTS

¼ oz gelatine
2 tablespoons water
4 oz cooked chicken
2 hard-boiled eggs
7 fl oz chicken stock
2 oz cooked peas

THE HOTEL METROPOLE

The Hotel Metropole, Minehead, shown in this postcard (issued by J. Stevens, Strand Promenade, Minehead, in the 1930s), headed the long list of hotels offering holiday accommodation. The Wellington, Holloway, Avalon, Merton and Granville had similar facilities, but on a smaller scale. Boarding terms in the late 1930s were from 25s 6d a day, or 168s a week. From the Hotel Metropole, there was a vista of Esplanade, bay and the buildings on North Hill. It can be clearly seen in a postcard issued in the 1950s and sent all over Britain; one recipient was Commander Browning of Dawlish, Devon.

Old Duck

METHOD
Dust the cleaned duck with seasoned flour, and brown in the heated butter. Pour off fat and add sherry, stock and herbs. Season to taste and simmer for an hour. Add the peas and cook on for another hour at a steady simmer. The beaten egg and cream are stirred in at the end and not allowed to boil. This sauce is served with the duck and peas. The tablespoon of freshly chopped mint is scattered over.

INGREDIENTS

3½–4 lb duck
salt and pepper
2 oz butter
2 tablespoons sherry
1 oz seasoned flour
1 lb freshly shelled peas
1 tablespoon chopped fresh mint
1 egg yolk, beaten in
1 tablespoon of thin cream
1 pint stock
1 teaspoon chopped fresh herbs

Roast Gliny

METHOD

The prepared guinea fowl should be stuffed with forcemeat or a bunch of herbs, with half a lemon placed in the cavity. Place in a roasting tin and cover the breast of the bird closely with the rashers of bacon (without these the fowl tends to be dry). Cook for half an hour in a moderate oven. Gently warm together the stock and the cider. Pour it over the bird in the roasting tin and cook for another 30 minutes, basting well. Keeping the bird warm, reduce the stock from the tin by fierce boiling in a pan. Remove from stove and add the cream. Gently warm again and it will be ready to serve with the carved fowl.

INGREDIENTS

1 plump guinea fowl
½ pint dry cider
¼ pint thick cream
enough bacon rashers to cover bird
seasoning
½ pint stock

THE BATTLE OF SEDGEMOOR

From the top of North Hill you can see Minehead, the harbour, the Dunster Hills, the long line of the Quantocks, and the coast past Burnham's white lighthouse to Weston-super-Mare and the Mendip Hills. On 5 July 1685, the Battle of Sedgemoor was fought at the village of Weston Zoyland – the area that became the nucleus of modern Weston. West Zoyland's church was filled with 500 dying and wounded royalists. For many years after the battle, the communal grave at Bissex was opened up during fairs, probably to teach the country folk a lesson. This fine September 1910 photograph of Weston-super-Mare's Old Pier shows steamboats, a mineral waters stand, and a water chute on the pier.

Nut Roast

METHOD

Chop nuts finely and heat the butter in a frying pan.
Grate the onion and put it in the frying pan with
the nuts. Fry for 3 minutes. Stir in the breadcrumbs,
seasoning and tomato ketchup. Add the beaten
egg and mashed potato, then mix all well together
with the stock. Turn into a buttered dish. Bake in a
moderate oven for 25 minutes, until brown. Thinly
sliced ripe tomatoes are good with hot nut roast.

INGREDIENTS

8 oz shelled nuts
1 medium-sized onion
6 oz breadcrumbs
1 dessertspoon tomato
  ketchup
1 oz butter
1 cup mashed potatoes
1 egg
2 tablespoons vegetable
  stock
salt and pepper

BOSSINGTON

The beautiful village of Bossington was a favoured haunt of artists, who came to paint the old thatched cottages and enormous walnut trees. Not far away were the ruins of East Myne farmhouse and the earthwork Bury Castle. This postcard, marked 11 August 1920, was written from 97 Bampton Street, Minehead, after a walk to Bossington, Allerford and Selworthy. The correspondent took the zig-zag road through the pines onto the moor. Deep, precipitous combes led down to the sea and visitors were warned of the dangers. An abbot of Athelney built the fifteenth-century chapel of Lynch, which, as the years passed, became a barn for storing grain until Sir Thomas Acland restored it fittingly as a chapel of ease in 1884. From here the visitor could climb Bossington Hill.

Meatless Shepherd's Pie

METHOD

Wash the lentils thoroughly and put them into a saucepan with the garlic, onion, herbs and pepper. Cover with 1½ pints of water. Bring to the boil, cover and simmer for 12 minutes. Drain off all the cooking liquid and mash the lentils. Add the tomatoes, tomato purée, courgettes, wheat germ and peppers. Warm gently for 5 minutes then add the parsley. Meanwhile, cook the potatoes in boiling water for 15 minutes. Drain and mash with half an ounce of margarine, a tablespoon of milk and the seasoning. Pile the mashed potato on top of the lentil mixture. Pattern the top with a fork and dot with the remaining margarine. Place under the grill for 15 minutes until browned.

INGREDIENTS

5 oz lentils
1 large onion, skinned and chopped
3 cloves garlic, crushed
2 teaspoons mixed herbs
salt and pepper
1¼ lb potatoes, peeled and chopped into large, even pieces
1½ oz margarine
1 tin chopped tomatoes
4 oz courgettes, sliced
2 oz wheat germ
5 oz mixed peppers, roughly chopped
3 tablespoons tomato purée
1 tablespoon chopped fresh parsley

WELLINGTON SQUARE, MINEHEAD

On the immediate right of this 1920s postcard issued by J. Stevens is the Plume and Feathers. There is very little traffic in the town, but 'sit-up-and-beg bicycles' with wicker baskets on the front were obviously useful for shopping. Behind the group of three is what appears to be the London City and Minehead Bank, with the grocer's shop next door. The Wellington Inn, on the corner of Bampton Street where it met Park Street, was diagonally across from the Plume of Feathers. Both were considered 'hotels' some twenty or thirty years later.

Bratton Gruel

Sailors' gruel was known as loblolly. The surgeon's assistant at sea was known as the loblolly boy.

METHOD
Mix the oatmeal to a thin paste with a little water. Put the milk in a saucepan with the remainder of the water and bring to the boil. Pour in the oatmeal and again bring to boiling point. The gruel should then be simmered gently for half an hour. Add the salt and sugar. A little cream makes the gruel smoother. To give colour and interest, sliced fresh strawberries could be dotted on the surface.

INGREDIENTS

1 oz fine oatmeal
½ pint milk
½ pint water
pinches of salt and sugar to taste
1 teaspoon cream
½ lb sliced strawberries

MINEHEAD, CAMP HILL AND BRATTON

This is Ted Lees in 1910. He attended the camp at Minehead that year, and worked with horses. A stretch of open moorland beyond pine plantations led to Camp Hill, where, in summer, Territorials came for annual training and were under canvas during their stay. Not far away was the village of Bratton, just 1½ miles from Minehead. Bratton Court, birthplace of a famous judge in the reign of Henry III, was visited by archaeologists and artists. The latter came to paint the picturesque cottages. Almost the whole of North Hill was open to the public for walks; that to Bratton is one excellent example.

Winter Broth

METHOD

Wash the leeks thoroughly and scald under boiling water. Cut them into pieces about an inch long – the green parts as well as the white. Put the meat and half of the leeks into the pot and simmer for half an hour; add the remaining leeks and continue to simmer for 3 hours. Skim carefully and season. It makes 4 quarts of broth and was probably consumed by family and farmworkers around a deal table. Quantities can be adjusted. It is a basic broth allowing for the addition of pulses and more vegetables. Some of today's packaged herbs and spice mixtures or a simple bouquet garni add more flavour.

INGREDIENTS

3 lb beef
10 large leeks
salt and pepper

VELLOW POTTERY

Thirty years ago we visited Vellow Pottery to watch the making of some lovely, traditional cooking pots, which we purchased. It was a pleasure to discover the kiln still active and the 'throwing' continuing. We also came across a Kohlangaz Fire Range, made especially by F. Manly of Skipton to take beautifully shaped terracotta ovenware. We tried out the recipe for winter broth in such a pot, with excellent results. Back at home, it was sole occupant of our electric oven. The recipe also is suitably old, dating from 1898.

Early Summer Hotch Potch

METHOD
The young vegetables should be washed, the carrots
and turnips cut small, the lettuce pulled apart leaf by
leaf, and the shallot onions chopped well – including
the green tops. Put all, with parsley and thyme,
into the mutton stock and simmer for half an hour.
Then add the peas and the washed white part of
cauliflower, broken into small, dainty sprigs.

INGREDIENTS

1 quart mutton stock
1 lettuce, cabbage-shaped
6 spring onions
4 young carrots
2 young turnips
1 small cauliflower
1 cup freshly shelled peas
1 sprig fresh parsley
1 sprig thyme

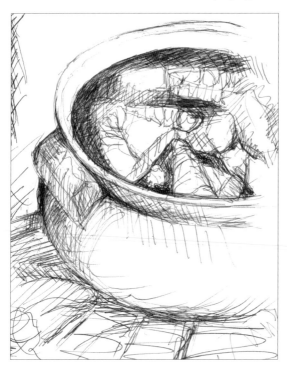

Simmer until these also are
cooked. The whole process takes
about an hour. Season towards
the end. The old way was to put
left-over meat from the joint into
the hotch potch a few minutes
before serving, but it is not now
considered advisable to warm
up meat in this way. The young
vegetables are a wonderful treat in
themselves.

PUNKIES

On the last Thursday of October at Hinton St George, children beg for candles
in the village and place them in hollowed large turnips or mangel-wurzels. The
lanterns are carved to represent faces, houses or trees. The children parade with
the 'punkies' held aloft and sing traditional songs, which are almost certainly
linked to the Samain, i.e. the Celtic fire rituals of 1 November.

Sheep's Head Soup

METHOD

The head should be washed very well and left to soak in warm, boiled water for an hour. Remove brains and tongue. Put the head in a large pan with the bunch of herbs, the vegetables (all cleaned and chopped), a teaspoon of coarse salt, and a sprinkling of black pepper. Add 3 pints of water and bring to the boil. Skim and simmer steadily for 2 hours. Meanwhile, wash the brains, removing any fibre, and boil gently in slightly salted water for 15 minutes. Pound them, mixing with butter and a few breadcrumbs. Stir this into the soup and simmer on for 1½ hours. Remove the meat from the head and put back into the soup, which will now be ready to serve. The tongue can be cooked along with the head, then skinned and used as a separate dish.

INGREDIENTS

INGREDIENTS
1 sheep's head
a bunch of fresh herbs
1 carrot
1 turnip
1 large Spanish onion
1 small piece celery
a few stalks of parsley
1 oz butter
1 tablespoon fine oatmeal
2 teaspoons pre-soaked barley
1 teaspoon tarragon vinegar
coarse salt and black pepper

Partridge Soup

METHOD

Skin partridges and cut into pieces. Fry with slices of ham, celery and onions in butter until brown. Put into a stew pan with water, a few peppercorns and a shank of mutton. Stew gently for 2 hours, then strain through a sieve. Put it back into stew pan, and, when really hot, pour into a tureen to serve.

INGREDIENTS

2 partridges
4 slices ham
4 stalks scrubbed celery
3 large, sliced onions
4oz butter
peppercorns
shank of mutton

SHOPPING IN MINEHEAD

This interesting early postcard of the Parade and Market House, Minehead, shows G. Brown's – a watchmaker and jeweller. Entering the business area by the picturesque Avenue, the visitor passed the Methodist Church and the Minehead and West Somerset Hospital. The Avenue led into the Parade, the main shopping centre, where there was also Market House, with its daily markets, and the county library. From the Parade was Bancks Street, which contained the Masonic Hall. The absence of traffic is amazing to modern eyes. People stand in what was then the main street, and the only vehicle is a horse-drawn carriage. Awnings over the shops indicate a warm, sunny day, but how quiet it looks!

Vegetable Soup

METHOD
The cucumbers and lettuce hearts should be pared and sliced, then placed into a saucepan with the fresh butter and stewed gently for half an hour. Then pour 2 quarts of boiling water onto the vegetables and stew for 2¼ hours. Before serving, add a little flour and water to thicken. Very small suet dumplings boiled in water were served with this early Victorian soup.

INGREDIENTS

5 cucumbers
5 lettuce hearts
2 sprigs of mint
3 small onions
1 lb young peas
salt and pepper
small quantity of parsley
½ lb fresh butter
1 tablespoon plain flour

Old-Fashioned Vegetable Soup from Crowcombe

METHOD
Brown the vegetables in the butter, then place them in the boiling water and cook for 45 minutes at a simmer. Add the oatmeal and boil again for another 10 minutes. Adjust seasoning to taste.

INGREDIENTS

1 tablespoon oatmeal
1 cup chopped onion
1 cup chopped carrot
½ cup chopped celery
2 tablespoons butter
3 pints boiling water

Stogumber Celery Soup

METHOD
Wash and chop the celery hearts. Slice up the potatoes
and onion. Cook them very slowly in the heated
butter until it is softened a little. Put in seasoning and
spice and mix well. Next add the stock and slowly
bring all to the boil, then set to simmer for ¾ of an
hour. Sieve the soup and add the cream, after which
reheat gently but on no account boil. Serve with the
chives floating on top. As in Devon and Kent, we
found that celery soup is a trusty favourite among
older people, 'to keep off the rheumatiz'.

INGREDIENTS

2 celery hearts
1 medium sliced onion
2 oz butter
½ pint cream
2 pints homemade
   chicken stock
2 tablespoons chopped
   chives
2 medium peeled
   potatoes
a pinch of nutmeg
freshly ground black
   peppercorns

THE STOGUMBER CANNONBALL

Legend says that guests assembled at
Stogumber church for the wedding of Elizabeth
Sydenham were startled by a flash and a hurtling cannon ball dropped at the feet
of the bride. Not surprisingly, Elizabeth took this as an omen and called off the
wedding. In 1585 she married Sir Francis Drake instead.

Egg Poached in Cream

METHOD
Butter a small ramekin and put in the cream.
Carefully break the egg into the cream, and sprinkle
with salt and pepper. Stand the ramekin in a small
pan containing water halfway up the side of the
dish. Simmer very gently until the egg is set. A little
grated Cheddar cheese on top of the egg makes a
pleasant change.

INGREDIENTS

1 egg
1 oz butter
2 tablespoons fresh cream
seasoning

River Trout Poached in Red Wine

METHOD

Thinly slice the onions and peeled lemons with a sharp knife and place on top of the washed trout in a deep pan. Season with salt and pepper. Heat the wine, adding sufficient water to cover the trout. Bring to the boil, then gently poach for 15 minutes. Brush with melted butter and serve with lemon slices.

INGREDIENTS

1 lb fresh trout
1 glass red wine
2 lemons
1 onion
salt and pepper

DULVERTON

The chief town of Exmoor, pictured here in 1934, was famous among stag hunters and fishermen worldwide. The River Barle rushes through to meet the Exe. Visitors came to enjoy the glorious views. It was frequently mentioned in R. D. Blackmore's *Lorna Doone*, which also helped to make the area famous. Lovers of the novel sought out the places associated with Lorna and hero John Ridd: Oare Church, Badgworthy Water, Malmsmead, Porlock. Dulverton was the home of 'Uncle Huckaback'. The postcard from 1919 shows the lych gate and an early perpendicular church situated near Dulverton station. The interesting, primitive stone causeway, the Tarr Steps, was 'not to be missed' by tourists, according to a county guidebook. The 180-foot-long bridge consists of huge slabs of stone 7 feet by 3 feet and the great stone piers are protected by large slabs 4 feet long.

Kedgeree

METHOD

Cook the rice in boiling water for 45 minutes until tender. Run cold water through it and drain. Place the haddock in a saucepan with ground pepper, bay leaf and sliced onions. Cover with cold water and simmer for 5 minutes. Lift out the fish, flake it and remove the core and seeds from the peppers and cut them into thin strips. In a large frying pan, heat the olive oil on a low heat and place in the peppers and thinly sliced onions, which should be cooked until soft. Mix in the fish, sultanas and curry powder and stir all together on a gentle heat for 5 minutes to bring out the flavours. The soured cream is spread around the edges of the serving dish.

INGREDIENTS

10 oz long grain brown rice
1½ lb smoked haddock
1 sliced onion
1 bay leaf
2 green peppers
4 tablespoons olive oil
1 thinly sliced large onion
2 oz sultanas
2 tablespoons curry power
¼ pint soured cream
ground pepper

SPORT IN MINEHEAD

Minehead Lawn Tennis Club off Alexandra Road, with grass and hard courts, charged 2s per hour per court in the 1930s. This group of visitors from 1909 appear to have only one racquet between them. Minehead and West Somerset Golf Club and Minehead Ladies' Golf Club offered an eighteen-hole course, with the fee for the visitors' green only 5s per day. Visitors were also welcomed to the Minehead Cricket Club, which played on the recreation ground. 1s per session covered the Minehead Bowling Club's charge in Irnham Road. Many came for the fishing alone, as the Exmoor rivers Exe and Barle offered excellent

angling. Tickets and licences could be obtained in Minehead. During the sea-fishing season, June to September, rock, whiting, codling, conger eels and thornbacks were the principal catches.

Cod Fish Cakes

METHOD

Good Somerset fish cakes are made with equal amounts of mashed potato and flaked cod. Mix the flaked fish with the potato, then mash it all up with the chives and seasoning. Shape into fish cakes, using a little flour. Brush with the beaten egg and scatter on the breadcrumbs. Fry in corn oil until golden on both sides.

They were often served with chopped turnips mashed up in cream.

INGREDIENTS

8 oz cooked cod
8 oz mashed potato
1 tablespoon chopped
  chives
seasoning
1 beaten egg
1 oz breadcrumbs

MINEHEAD QUAY

In the 1930s, donkeys were used to climb the steep street up to the church in Minehead. Minehead's North Hill inspired the artist Turner to paint one of his greatest pictures and Daniel Defoe visited in the days when ships from Minehead's quay traded as far away as Portugal, North America and Africa. As the sea fell back, the quay was extended, the result being the safest harbour on the coast. Today's town has not only the large holiday camp at Warren Road by the golf course, but also a miniature railway. Fishing trips continue to be popular and horses can be hired.

Church Town Minehead.

Crab with Anchovy

METHOD
Pound the anchovies in a bowl. Add the breadcrumbs, stock and basil and bring to boil. Simmer for 4 minutes. Mix the crab with the butter and add to the warmed anchovies etc. Cook for
5 minutes, stirring well, and serve in scallop shells with buttered wholemeal toast.

INGREDIENTS

meat of 2 medium-sized crabs
a pinch of basil
3 anchovy fillets
salt and pepper
3 tablespoons wholemeal breadcrumbs
2 oz butter
¼ pint fish stock

MINEHEAD QUAY

At Minehead Quay, in a very old oak-beamed house once known as Gibraltar Cellar, were the 'inner sellers'. It was used as a timber store until it was purchased by a Minehead vicar and made into a chapel for the ancient Quay Town – the old part of Minehead. The inscription outside the chapel of St. Peter's, adjoining the Pier Hotel, explained that Holy Eucharist was offered every Friday at 8 a.m. for the benefit of sailors about to put to sea ('God speed the ship'). Quay Town, though modernised, is still picturesque, with its fishermen's cottages clustered along the street at the foot of North Hill. This postcard, from 1925, shows the Quay Promenade.

Crab Salad

This salad was served sixty years ago at Ilfracombe, where my mother went for several years with a factory party.

METHOD

Wash the rice and cook it in boiling water with a teaspoon of salt and the vinegar. Strain after 15 minutes, separate grains and allow to cool. Take all the meat from the cooked crab and flake it. Mix together the mustard, mayonnaise and sauce. Add the crab meat, rice and cream. Season all with the salt, cayenne and lemon juice. Take a large lettuce, wash it well, and dry the leaves. Place heaps of the crab mixture on the largest leaves. With the tiny tender leaves of lettuce, make a pattern to set off the delicate meat and serve in the crab shell.

INGREDIENTS

1 large crab
½ gill mayonnaise
½ teaspoon mustard mixed with cream
1 dessertspoon Worcester sauce
salt and cayenne pepper
juice of ½ lemon
1 tablespoon cream
2 oz freshly boiled rice
1 tablespoon tarragon vinegar

THE WRECK OF THE *FORREST HALL*

Thousands of these stylised cards, 'Waiting for the Boats', were sent out from the West Country; this one dates from 1904. A sou'westered coxswain like this fisherman was used on posters of the Royal National Lifeboat Institution to appeal for funds. Fishermen, lifeboatmen and sailors were frequently drowned.

A lifeboat was once kept at Minehead, but it was found more satisfactory to launch a motor boat from Porlock Weir. Of all the exciting and demanding incidents at sea, none could be more dramatic than the wreck of the *Forrest Hall*. The sailing ship was crippled off Porlock in January 1899. Eighteen horses hauled the lifeboat *Louisa* up Countisbury Hill and over Exmoor. Launching at Lynmouth not being possible, they made for Porlock Weir. En route they had to put the lifeboat on skids and partially demolish a cottage to get it past. 10½ hours later, on Friday the 13th at 6.30 a.m., *Louisa* was launched. The supermen on board were all volunteers.

Stewed Eels

METHOD

Toss eel in flour that has been seasoned with salt and pepper. Heat oil in a stew pan and brown the eel pieces. Remove eel and sauté onion. Put back the eel slices, add mushrooms, wine and seasoning, and simmer for 30 minutes or until tender. Knead butter and flour together and thicken the eel liquor with this by adding small pieces gradually, stirring all the time. You will feel the sauce thicken smoothly. Serve with the lemon slices as garnish.

INGREDIENTS

3 lb skinned eels cut up
4 tablespoons oil
20 button mushrooms
1 pint red wine
6 oz chopped, skinned onions
freshly ground sea salt
black pepper
seasoned flour
1 tablespoon flour
1 tablespoon soft butter
lemon slices

MINEHEAD HARBOUR

Minehead Harbour, dating from 1616, has been considerably extended. In the early seventeenth century there was much trade with Ireland.

Indeed, one of the town's trusts, the Cow Charity, originated in the importation of cattle from Ireland, which was forbidden in Charles II's reign. A large number of beasts arriving in 1669 were seized at the port of Minehead and sold, and the money was invested in land. Annual rents were entered by the churchwardens in a book called the Cow Money Book and the charity then dispensed to those in need. This photograph shows the harbour in August 1956. Boats could be hired and a day's fishing arranged, usually with fishermen from the cottages. Conger eels caught here were reputed to be of enormous size. There used to be a promenade pier, 250 feet in length, but it was demolished during the Second World War.

Baked Aubergines

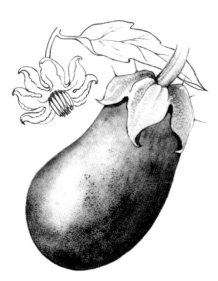

INGREDIENTS

4 aubergines
1 dessertspoon salt
2 oz butter

METHOD
Peel and slice the aubergines. Sprinkle
salt over them. Leave for 20 minutes
to drain off any bitterness. Drain and
place in a fireproof dish. Dot with butter.
Cover and bake for half an hour at
400 °F. Serve with a favourite sauce.

Cheddar Cheese Dumplings

*These 'dough boys' are sustaining on cold
winter days. Almost the same recipe was given
when we met ladies in Dunster, only they were
named 'Cheddar Dough Boys'.*

METHOD
Mix the dry ingredients together and then
mix them with the water to produce a soft
but not over-wet dough. Shape into little
balls with floured hands. Toss into soup in
the last half-hour of cooking.

INGREDIENTS

2 oz finely grated
   Cheddar cheese
seasoning
4 oz plain flour
½ teaspoon baking
   powder
2 oz shredded suet
a small pinch of
   marjoram

DUNSTER

The name Dunster is derived
from 'Dun', a hill and tor (i.e. a
tower). In Saxon lord Aluric's
time, it was known as Dunestorre.
William de Mohun extended
the great fortress and it became
one of the most important in
the west of England. The village
remains unspoiled, much as it
was in feudal times over 600
years ago, although the only link
with the original castle is the
thirteenth-century gateway built
by Reginald de Mohun. This
beautiful study by Judges shows

the castle, the village street, the Yarn Market erected by George Luttrell in 1609,
and the Luttrell Arms on the left. The 'kerseymeres', or 'dunsters', were sold at the
yarn market when the town was famous for its woollen cloth.

It is still the custom at the Luttrell Arms, Dunster, to burn a faggot or bundle
of twelve ash branches in the great fireplace. This has been done since medieval
times. As each ashband binding the faggot burns through, another round of hot
punch is ordered from the bar. As the wood burns, the Dunster Carol is sung.
When the last bit is consumed, a fragment is taken out to light the next year's
fire. Burning the Ashen Faggot was once a widespread Somerset custom on
Christmas Eve.

In the 1920s photograph (left), the Old
Nunnery can be seen, although the name is
misleading. Until the nineteenth century the
building was called High House and documents
at Dunster Castle describe it as 'the tenement of
Saint Laurence'. It is sited in Church Street, at
right angles to High Street, and has a slated roof
and three overhanging storeys. Centuries ago the
village corn was ground at the Old Mill, or 'Grist
Mill', near Church Street. By the 1940s it was
grinding cattle food. Packhorse Bridge, alongside
the mill, was a well-known beauty spot leading
to Gallows Hill, where Judge Jeffreys hanged the
supporters of the Monmouth Rebellion.

Somerset Herb Cheese

An old Somerset custom is called 'bringing in the bread and cheese'. A huge loaf and a huge cheese are borne in on the shoulders of farmworkers.

METHOD
Grate the cheese and mix with the other ingredients. Render it down in a double saucepan, stirring all the time for maximum creaminess. Pour into small pots and cool. The herbs make it a delicate green-blue colour.

INGREDIENTS

1 lb Cheddar cheese
2 tablespoons chopped chives
6 tablespoons cream
parsley

CHEDDAR GORGE

Lion Rock and Cheddar Gorge are the subject of this study from 1910. The former towers over the village of Cheddar, which lies a mile from the famous Cheddar Gorge. People came from Minehead to see both and usually fitted in a visit to the Wookey Hole Caves, where ran the subterranean River Axe. As far back as 1511, the caverns were known as Cheddarhole. Due to the boom in tourism, Gough's Cave and Cox's Cave have been fitted with lights to show the beauty of the stalactites and stalagmites that have built up over the ages. Edward VII was one famous visitor. The skeleton of a Palaeolithic man – as well as flint tools, Roman coins and bone implements – were discovered in one cave. The caves were rediscovered between 1837 and 1893. The Mendip Hills are honeycombed with a system of caves, some of which have never been explored. Of the 600 caves visited by Monsieur Martel of Paris in the early 1900s, he admired Cox's the most.

Tossed Spring Salad

METHOD
Wash. Chop onions and cucumber and place watercress in a dish. Toss the salad in the dressing.

INGREDIENTS

a bunch of watercress
a little cucumber
spring onions

For the dressing:
1½ tablespoons olive oil
½ tablespoon vinegar
a little pepper and salt
a pinch of dry mustard

SOMERSET LAVENDER

The local lavender grows into huge bushes in places like Watchet, Minehead, Blue Anchor, Porlock, Old Cleeve and Wootton Courtenay. It was so prolific that bags and pillows could be stuffed with flowers which scented chests, wardrobes, drawers and presses, or went into bowls of potpourri.

Baking

Milk Cottage Loaves

A sixty-year-old recipe, but quick and useful today.

METHOD
Grease a baking sheet and pre-heat the oven to 400 °F.
Sift the flour and salt and rub in butter. Add baking
powder and mix well. Beat the egg and milk, keeping
back a little for glazing. Mix very quickly. Do not
knead. Cut the dough into 16 pieces. Shape all the
pieces into 'rounds' and moisten the top of the large
pieces with a little water. Put the small rounds onto
the big, pressing them down centrally with the
little finger. Do this as quickly as possible. Brush
over with the glaze and get the cottage loaves into
the oven on the baking sheet. 15 minutes in a hot oven cooks them.

INGREDIENTS

1 lb flour
2 oz butter
1 egg
1 teaspoon salt
½ pint milk
2 teaspoons baking
   powder

J. G. HOUGHTON
1966

Farm Bread

METHOD

Soak the sultanas in tea overnight. Add egg,
self-raising flour and Demerara sugar. Mix well and
pour into an oblong, greased tin. Bake at 350 °F for
30 minutes. Eat hot with butter.

> INGREDIENTS
>
> 1 cup washed sultanas
> 1 beaten egg
> 2 teacups self-raising
>   flour
> 1 cup Demerara sugar
> tea

LUCCOMBE

John de Luccombe lent his name to the Somerset
village of Luccombe. Locally, the area was once known
as 'the courting valley'. It is worth visiting for its picturesque cream-and-pink-
painted thatched cottages and interesting bread ovens with tall chimneys. There is
one in Stony Street dating from the seventeenth century. This village is made more
picturesque by the stream flowing through it; its source is Dunkery Hill.

There are further examples of the seventeenth-century bread ovens at
Allerford, which has a fine example of an eighteenth-century bridge, built with
sufficient width to accommodate trains of heavily laden pack horses.

Sally Lunns

*Even though it was wartime, the Sally Lunns my sister
and I had in Bath over forty years ago were richer in
ingredients than those of this recipe. The sad-looking
Pump Room was closed and the enemy had directly hit
the centre of the Royal Crescent. These golden yeasty
cakes are still made in Bath. The name derives from old
French – a corruption of soleil (sun) and lune (moon).*

> INGREDIENTS
>
> 1 lb flour
> 2 oz butter
> 1 egg
> 1 oz sugar
> a pinch of salt
> 1 oz yeast
> 1 teaspoon caster sugar
> ½ pint lukewarm milk

METHOD

Mix the sugar and the salt with the flour. Rub in the
butter. With the caster sugar, cream the yeast and
add a tablespoon of milk. Allow to stand in a warm
place for 10 minutes then add it to the well in the
flour. Mix in half the flour, then put in the beaten
egg and mix with the milk to a soft dough.

Grease eight large patty tins. Knead the dough very well and place portions of it in
the tins, but only half fill them. Leave in a warm place till the dough has doubled in
size. Bake in a hot oven for 20 minutes.

BATH AND WELLS

Of the many trips that visitors staying at Minehead were encouraged to make, two were to the cities of Bath and Wells in order to see the Abbey and Cathedral respectively.

The son of Alfred the Great, Edward the Elder founded the bishopric of Wells in AD 909. The Dean's Eye, the fifteenth-century gateway in Sadler Street, leading out of Market Place, was deemed the best approach onto the broad lawn and the magnificent west front with its many statues. The chapter house and old clock, made in 1325, have been drawing visitors for many years.

At Wells in 1451, a well or 'conduit house' was constructed alongside St Andrew's Well, where a spring of fresh water arose. It was designed to carry drinking water under the cloister and out into the market place. Another manorial officer was the wellmaster, who was responsible for adequate and clean water supply.

This postcard from 1912 shows the Grand Pump Room and the Abbey at Bath, with the Mutual Life Company of New York on the left.

John Palmer, who was painted by Gainsborough, received the freedom of eighteen cities and represented Bath in Parliament from 1801 to 1807. He was eventually buried in Bath Abbey, his great service to the country being the establishment of mail coaches. As a young man managing his father's theatres, he had to travel in order to find performers and he dreamed of a network of mail coaches that could quickly cover the entire land. The Post Office was his worst enemy, but he succeeded and became wealthy. The photograph overleaf shows the original Bath Mail Coach. The Royal Arms were emblazoned on the deep maroon door panels and the royal cypher was in gold on the rear boot. These were undisputed kings of the road, paying no tolls and claiming right of way.

In the early nineteenth century, 342 coaches left London daily for country places. The Bath Mail Coach ran to such a tight schedule that at some post offices on the way, the mail bag was adroitly passed from an open window of the post office without the coach having to stop. Only 20 minutes was allowed for refreshment (breakfast or dinner), and passengers were usually so ravenous on arrival at the coaching inns that behaviour was unruly. Indeed, the real test of a gentleman in those days was whether he escorted the ladies from the coach. Famous inns, open 24 hours a day, provided refreshment and rest for passengers and stabling for horses.

Hot Cross Buns

METHOD

Melt the honey with the hot water. Add enough cold milk to make up a pint and to this smooth in the yeast. Place in a warm but not hot position. Next, rub the fat into the flour, spice and salt. Stir in the lukewarm yeast mixture and knead the dough produced. Cover and set it to rise in a warm place for 2 hours. You could meanwhile make a little pastry, which will be necessary for marking the buns with a cross.

After 2 hours, when the dough will have doubled in size by the yeast action, stir in the dried fruit and roll into twelve balls, which should be gently flattened. Cut strips of pastry and place in cruciform fashion on each bun. Brush the tops with whisked egg yolk.

INGREDIENTS

1 lb strong white flour
1 teaspoon allspice
¼ pint milk
2 oz butter
1½ tablespoons honey
¼ pint hot water
6 oz dried fruit (currants, raisins, peel)
1 oz fresh yeast
½ teaspoon freshly ground sea salt
egg yolk
pastry strips (see page 88)

Somerset Scones

METHOD

Sift flour and salt into a bowl and add baking powder. Rub in the butter until the mixture resembles breadcrumbs and beat in the eggs with the cream. A little milk may also be necessary to produce a firm, clean dough. Knead well, then roll out and cut into rounds. Bake in a hot oven for 15 minutes until golden brown.

INGREDIENTS

2 lb flour
1 teaspoon salt
3 teaspoons baking powder
3 oz butter
3 oz cream
2 eggs

These plain scones were cut in half fresh from the oven and served with homemade jam and lots of clotted cream. Old recipes often have large quantities, as families and farmhands had to be fed. Half quantities might suffice, as scones need to be made in fresh batches frequently.

THE CLIFTON SUSPENSION BRIDGE

It has a span of 702 feet and is suspended 245 feet above the Avon river gorge. The graceful Clifton Suspension Bridge was opened in 1864 and designer Isambard Kingdom Brunel called it his 'darling' and his 'first child'. One of the famous 'paddlers' that made trips up to Minehead, the steamer *Gwalia*, is in this photograph.

Somerset Wheatmeal Scones

METHOD
Sieve the plain flour and add the other dry
ingredients. Rub in the butter and by adding a little
milk give the mixture a soft consistency that can be
rolled out on a floured board and cut into rounds.
Bake in an oven at 400 °F for 15 minutes until the
scones are slightly browned.

INGREDIENTS

¼ lb plain flour
¼ lb wheatflour
½ oz butter
1 tablespoon caster sugar
½ teaspoon bicarbonate
of soda
¾ teaspoon salt
a little milk

Cheese Straws

METHOD
Mix as you would pastry, i.e. by rubbing margarine
into flour until it looks like breadcrumbs. Add the
grated cheese and salt. Use the egg yolk to bind. Roll
out and cut into strips. Bake for 20 minutes at 400 °F.

INGREDIENTS

8 oz plain flour
4 oz margarine
2 oz grated cheese
pinch of sea salt
1 egg yolk, whisked up

SYCAMORE HOUSE

The three-storey house at the foot of Jacob's Ladder,
Cheddar, was run by the Pavey family, whose
luncheons and teas were most acceptable after scaling
the heights. Outside Sycamore House in 1934 stood
an old-fashioned ice cream barrow selling delicious
homemade cornets and wafers. I recall a 'Cheddar
Cheese Depot' opposite, from where visitors could
send cheeses home. The few cars around in those
days had 'dickey seats', substantial running boards
and hoods that pulled back so that you could enjoy
the sunshine and the views. Neighbouring Draycott
was well known for strawberry-and-cream teas.
Ebbor Gorge, another ravine near Cheddar, could be
climbed by footpath. From 300 feet up, magnificent
views over three counties are laid out before you.

Jacob's Ladder, Cheddar, Somerset.

Traditional Boiled Fruit Cake

*This boiled fruit cake was suggested by a lady in
Porlock. The idea of boiling a cake was quite new to me.*

METHOD
Place all in a saucepan except the eggs and flour.
Bring to the boil and simmer for 6 minutes. Cool.
Stir in the eggs and flour. Line a cake tin with three
layers of greaseproof paper. Pour mixture into
tin and bake at 340 °F for 2 hours, lowering the
temperature a little towards the end of baking.

INGREDIENTS

12 oz raisins
3 oz shredded candied peel
6 oz Demerara sugar
½ pint milk
2 oz flaked almonds
4 oz butter
½ teaspoon mixed spice
2 eggs
12 oz flour
¼ teaspoon bicarbonate of soda

PORLOCK WEIR

Porlock's harbour was left high and dry in the
Middle Ages by retreating seas, but Porlock
Weir, having a bar of shingle to enclose a tidal
inlet, managed to become a small port. The dock has gates that enable craft to
stay afloat and is reached by a narrow channel. From here can be seen Hurlstone
Point and Bossington Hill. In the seventeenth century, herrings were landed. Salt
and limestone were once imported and cloth exported. Porlock cloth was also
sold at the Yarn Market, Dunster. At that time, the local people used primitive
sledges to descend Porlock Hill.

Somerset Rich Cake

The old-fashioned sugar/butter method has long been used for making rich fruit cakes. Oranges and lemons were traditionally added to give a distinct flavour, the citrus flavour being complemented by the sweetness of marzipan and icing sugar.

METHOD

Pre-heat oven to 300 °F. Grease and line a deep 9-inch cake tin. Cream the butter, sugar and treacle. Beat in the eggs one at a time, adding a tablespoon of the flour with the last two. Sieve in the remaining flour and spices. Stir in the nuts, the cleaned, dried fruit, and the lemon and orange rind. Turn the mixture into a prepared tin and smooth the top, hollowing slightly. Bake for 3–4 hours.

If icing is to be done, coat the cake with boiling apricot jam and leave it to dry for a week. Sprinkle rum over the base of the cake before icing it.

INGREDIENTS

8 oz butter
2 oz blanched, chopped almonds
8 oz soft brown sugar
3 oz mixed chopped peel
1 tablespoon treacle
4 oz glacé cherries
5 large eggs
6 oz sultanas
9 oz plain flour
6 oz raisins
1 teaspoon mixed spice
10 oz currants
½ teaspoon grated nutmeg
grated rind of a lemon
grated rind of an orange
apricot jam
2 tablespoons rum
icing sugar

Lemon Cake

METHOD
Preheat the oven to 350 °F. Butter a 2 lb loaf tin. Put
butter and sugar in a large bowl and beat well until
fluffy. Gradually beat in the eggs, followed by the
lemon zest (lime or orange zest could be used if
preferred). Sift the flour into the bowl and fold into
the cake mixture. Add the milk and mix all together
well. Spoon the mixture into the cake tin and bake
for 50 minutes until the cake is golden brown and
firm. Mix lemon juice and icing sugar together.
Spike small holes in the top of the cake and pour the
lemon and icing sugar mixture over the cake. Leave
it to set and cool before removing from the tin.

INGREDIENTS

6 oz butter
6 oz caster sugar
2 medium fresh eggs, beaten
grated zest and juice of a lemon
6 oz self-raising flour
2 tablespoons milk
1 tablespoon icing sugar

HALSWAY MANOR, CROWCOMBE

In August 1952 we stayed at Halsway Manor. It seemed the whole world was
soaked in sunshine and the scent of lavender. The sight of three flaxen-haired
children won me several recipes, and, from one Somerset lady, a verse even about
her cake:

> Pat it and prick it
> And mark it with B,
> Then put it in the oven
> For Benny and me.

Folklore, perhaps. Cecil Sharp was also visiting Somerset at the time, researching
songs and folk dancing for revival at Halsway Manor.

Chocolate Cake

METHOD

To the softened margarine add the syrup, flour, drinking chocolate and instant coffee. Mix in the two beaten eggs and lastly put in the cooled milk and bicarbonate of soda. Place the mixture in two loose-bottomed tins and bake for 25 minutes at 375 °F. When cool, the two cakes can be sandwiched together with 2 oz of melted dark chocolate.

INGREDIENTS

4 oz sugar
6 oz flour
4 oz margarine
2 well-beaten eggs
4 oz golden syrup
2 oz dark chocolate
2 oz drinking chocolate
½ teaspoon instant coffee
¼ pint warm milk
½ teaspoon bicarbonate
of soda

A BRISTOL COFFEE HOUSE

Among the rules of a certain Somerset coffee house in 1674 was, 'He that shall any quarrel here begin, shall give each man a dish to atone the sin.' Carwardines ('Coffee Roasters and Blenders since 1777') sold 'the finest souchong tea'. The company's Bristol coffee house was opened at 56 Corn Street in the 1920s to complement its flourishing tea and coffee business.

Farmhouse Fruit Cake

METHOD
Grease a round cake tin (diameter 8 inches) and set oven at 350 °F. Cream together margarine, honey and sugar. Beat in the eggs. Sift together flour, spices and baking powder and fold the dry ingredients into the mixture. Carefully add milk to produce a soft dropping consistency. Turn into the cake tin and smooth the top. Bake in the centre of the oven for 60 minutes.

INGREDIENTS

6 oz soft margarine
2 tablespoons honey
4 oz brown sugar
2 free-range eggs
10 oz mix of currants,
     sultanas and raisins
1 teaspoon mixed spice
½ teaspoon cinnamon
2 teaspoons baking
     powder
a little skimmed milk
8 oz wholemeal flour

Heavy Cake from Porlock

Sometimes called 'Heavy Cake' in other parts of the West Country.

METHOD
Mix salt with flour and rub in the fats. Beat in the egg and milk. Add spices, sugar, currants, raisins and sliced candied peel into a flat, round cake 2 inches thick. Place in a greased baking tin and bake in a moderate oven for half an hour.

INGREDIENTS
¼ lb flour
2 oz caster sugar
1 oz butter
1 oz lard
2 oz raisins
2 oz currants
pinch of cinnamon and nutmeg
1 egg
½ teaspoon mixed spice
1 tablespoon milk
pinch of salt
1 oz candied peel

PORLOCK

In the earlier years of the century, Porlock was a favourite hunting centre with riding schools and stabling facilities. Since Saxon times, hunting red deer and wolves was the sport of kings. Porlock market was important, and the Ship Inn is a reminder that Porlock was once a port, (the sea has since receded). The inn was visited by Robert Southey.

Porlock church, restored in 1890, is dedicated to St Dubricius, but its site is Saxon. It was supposedly built by Sir Simon Fitz-Roges, a thirteenth-century crusader whose interesting but damaged effigy can still be found inside. It is unusual on account of its massive tower and stumpy, octagonal steeple. In 1700, the original spire was destroyed in a gale. One of the most ancient clocks in England, in use for over 400 years, is sited near the belfry screen. The alabaster Harington monument, also one of the best in England, was restored in 1939 but still bears signs of disfigurement.

Nut Cake

This recipe is very similar to one I was given in Kitzbühel, Austria, and I suspect it originally flourished in forested areas with a good supply of hazelnuts in the autumn. In Austria they called it Esterhazy Schnitte. *Almonds are used when hazelnuts are not available.*

INGREDIENTS

white of 4 eggs
8 oz sugar
8 oz rubbed almonds or hazelnuts

METHOD

Whisk most of the egg white until it is stiff, then add the sugar and rubbed (i.e. finely chopped and blanched) almonds. Place in a buttered baking tin and cook in a moderate oven for about 30 minutes. Immediately after baking, cut the cake in broad slices. Stuff the slices with chopped glacé cherries. Glaze with the remaining egg white.

Molasses Cake

METHOD
Cream the margarine, adding the sugar slowly
and beating continuously. Add the beaten egg and
molasses (syrup or treacle). Add half of the flour with
baking powder, salt, soda and spices sifted together.
Add milk and the rest of the dry ingredients. Mix
well and bake in a greased, 2 inch deep tin in a
moderate oven for 40 minutes. This should be
served hot and was often used as pudding with a
cornflour sauce.

INGREDIENTS

2 cups margarine
½ cup brown sugar
½ cup molasses
1 egg
2 cups flour
3 teaspoons baking powder
¼ teaspoon bicarbonate
of soda
½ teaspoon allspice
1 teaspoon cinnamon
1 cup milk
¼ teaspoon salt

DUCHESS OF HAMILTON

Passing Blue Anchor on the Minehead branch
railway is ex-LMS Pacific No. 6229 *Duchess
of Hamilton*. She was being towed to Swindon for
repainting before going on to York to be on exhibition in the National Railway
Museum. Many holidaymakers would recognise her, as she was once the
locomotive at Butlin's Holiday Camp, Minehead. The photograph dates from the
early 1970s.

Hazelnut Shortcakes

METHOD
Mix flour with sugar. Mix in the chopped hazelnuts.
Knead in the butter until it becomes a soft dough and
roll it out half an inch thick. With a fluted cutter, or
using the floured rim of a teacup, cut into rounds
and top with a whole nut. A very moderate oven
(350 °F) is required. It should be just 20 minutes
before the shortcakes are golden brown.

INGREDIENTS

½ lb self-raising flour
3 oz caster sugar
3 oz finely chopped
hazelnuts
6 oz butter

Whortleberry Pie from Dunster

METHOD
Using a pastry made by rubbing the margarine into
the flour, fill the pie dish with whortleberries and
sprinkle with sugar to taste. Make a lid for the pie
with the remaining pastry and bake at 400 °F for
about half an hour.

INGREDIENTS
¾ lb whortleberries
sugar to taste

For the pastry:
5 oz margarine
8 oz flour

DUNSTER CHURCH

When the custom, which may still be observed, was for children to hold a rope across the church door on the occasion of a wedding, the bridegroom would approach, scattering a generous handful of coins for which the children scrambled, thereby dropping the rope and allowing entry to the church. My mother recalled this custom as 'perry werry'. On the death of a parishioner, the passing bell of Dunster church tolled the number of strokes corresponding to the age of the person being buried. Dunster church is pictured here in 1929. The church is dedicated to St George, and its warm, pink sandstone and sub-tropical plants are beautiful to see in the summer sun. The church was in existence by 1100. A group of monks was in residence here until 1539.

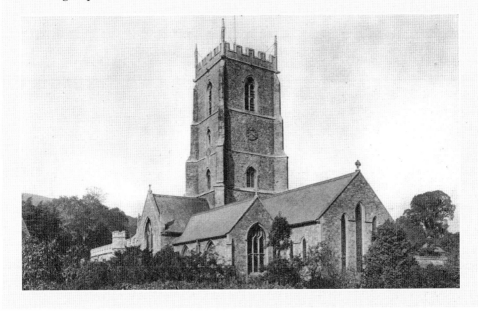

Mince Pie

METHOD

Rub margarine into flour until it resembles breadcrumbs. Make a well in the centre and add egg yolk, rum and cream. Mix all together until a pliable dough is formed. Place in the fridge for 10 minutes, then roll out pastry thinly. Cut into small rounds and line greased patty tins. Fill with mincemeat and place rounds on tops to form lids. Brush with beaten egg and bake in a hot oven (400 °F) until golden brown.

INGREDIENTS

5 oz flour
4 oz margarine
1 egg yolk
1 egg, beaten
1 teaspoon rum
1 tablespoon cream
1 lb mincemeat

Watchet Fig Pie

As in Devon and Cornwall, Somerset manages to grow figs out of doors on mellow walls. There is a huge, successful fig tree in the lea of Dunster Castle. The monks introduced figs long ago – they were first used medicinally, internally and externally. Fig gardens, although less numerous than strawberry gardens, were popular in Victorian times, and when the figs were ripe, customers could eat as many as they liked. Figgy Sunday (or Fig Pie Sunday) occurs in a number of regions. My father insisted on a pie filled with figs on that day and I distinctly recall a second fig pie date in November, when the soft fruits of the summer were over. The figs made a nice change from apples.

METHOD

Make the pastry by rubbing the lard into the flour. When it resembles breadcrumbs, bind carefully with iced water, adding it little by little (about 1½ tablespoons), but do not make the pastry soggy. Keep it cool while you prepare the figs, which will nowadays almost certainly be from packets. Wash the loosely-broken figs and then soak them in a little brandy for a while. Snip off any stalks. Drain and cut them into narrow strips. After rolling out the pastry, arrange the figs in the pie dish, adding a light scattering of sugar, then put on the lid and bake in a moderate oven until the pastry is golden brown. This quantity of pastry will make two medium-sized pies.

INGREDIENTS

2 packets (or 1 box) figs

For the pastry:
8 oz lard
16 oz flour

WATCHET

In the seventeenth century, the small port of Watchet on the River Washford, only eight miles from Minehead, produced paper. Its Celtic name means 'under the wood', the land rising behind having once been heavily wooded, as can be gleaned from documents at the record office. Welsh influence is evident in names like St Decuman, and trade with Wales dates back to the Middle Ages. In Saxon times Watchet had a mint and issued its own coins. On each side of the harbour there are cliffs veined with red-and-white alabaster, from which bookends and ash trays were being made in the 1930s. Holidaymakers loved the quayside activity.

In 1900, such was the ferocity of the sea that the harbour was nearly destroyed and shipping was heavily damaged. A great effort on the part of the townspeople rebuilt the harbour at a cost of £25,000. In our earlier visits, the Quantock Staghounds and West Somerset Foxhounds met near Watchet.

It is interesting to learn that Watchet became well known for its biscuits, which were enjoyed by both sailors and visitors. These were a superior kind of ship's biscuit, much better than 'the usual hard tack'. The flour for Watchet and Bridgwater Manchips was supplied locally by Messrs Stoate. Fatcakes and Manchips were consumed in large quantities on 'Caturn's Night'. A lady, Catherine, either a saint or a queen, once provided a feast of hot cakes and scrumpy or farmhouse cider, which later became a traditional event. Fatcakes – lardies stuffed with currants – resemble Cornwall's 'Heavy Cakes'.

In old Watchet, when the reeve, ale-taster, hayward and wellmaster were appointed at the court leet and sworn in, 'they all sat down to a hearty meal of roast goose, followed by hot punch and walnuts,' according to a record found preserved in the parish chest. The custom survived into the 1980s.

Bilberry Pie

METHOD
Make the pastry by rubbing the lard into the flour until it resembles breadcrumbs. Bind with half a gill of water. Use only the tips of your fingers and keeping everything cool, roll out the pastry. Line a deep pie dish and put in a generous pound of washed bilberries. Make a lid for the pie. Gently press down to cover the fruit – which should have had moist sugar added according to taste. Cook in a hot oven for half an hour.

INGREDIENTS

1 lb bilberries
sugar to taste

For the pastry:
4 oz lard
8 oz flour

THE GREAT WORM

Shervage Wood was once famous for bilberries, but a shepherd and two gypsies vanished while they were picking the berries and the legend of the Great Worm arose. One Crowcombe lady who made a living out of the pies could find no one to pick the bilberries until a woodman from Stogumber arrived. Seated on a log, drinking cider and eating cheese, the woodman suddenly felt the log writhe beneath him. Quick as a flash, he chopped off both ends. One end slithered off to Kingston St Mary and the other to Bilbrook, near Minehead, and that was the end of the Worm. Meanwhile, the woodman delivered a great hatful of bilberries to be made into pies.

Loganberry Sponge

METHOD

Put half the loganberries in a jar and stand this in boiling water over moderate heat to get the juice flowing. Drain off the juice and allow it to cool. Mix 2 tablespoons of the juice with 4 oz of the icing sugar. With the well-whipped cream, spread this in the middle of the sandwich cake. Whip the remaining icing sugar with the white of egg and spread this on top of the cake, then decorate it with whole loganberries.

To make the sponge, you need very fresh eggs and dry, sifted flour. Beat the sugar and butter to a very soft cream. Sift the flour. Beat the eggs for 10 minutes. Stir them into the creamed butter and mix very well. Add the flour a little at a time, beating constantly. Turn the sponge mixture, which should look rather like batter, into two floured sandwich tins and bake in a moderate oven for 40 minutes.

INGREDIENTS

1 lb loganberries
½ lb icing sugar
white of an egg
2 tablespoons thick cream

For the sponge sandwich:
4 oz plain flour
4 oz butter
4 oz caster sugar
2 eggs

BLUE ANCHOR BAY

High tide at Blue Anchor is shown on this 1920s postcard, which reveals the great sweep of bay, with Minehead in the distance. In the time of Edward IV, a chapel stood above Blue Anchor, but a landslip cast most of it into the bay. However, the image of the Virgin Mary remained on the cliff unharmed – a miraculous sign that led to King Edward granting a charter for a market. From the proceeds, a new chapel was built inland. A fine stone wall and promenade with safe bathing ensured the arrival of many daytrippers from Minehead, and the rocks plus the chance of finding fossils ensured a lovely day out.

Syrup Sponge

METHOD
Beat the egg well and place in mixing bowl. Add flour and bicarbonate of soda. Next stir in sugar and syrup, then add butter and pour over it the boiling water. Mix all ingredients well and when smooth, pour into a baking tin and bake at 340 °F for about an hour. More melted syrup over the pudding when serving makes it a children's delight, but make sure they clean their teeth well after this old, indulgent favourite.

INGREDIENTS

8 oz sifted self-raising flour
6 oz sugar
½ teaspoon bicarbonate of soda
1 egg
3 tablespoons golden syrup
5 oz butter
¼ pint boiling water

Rhubarb Sponge Pudding

This pudding is a favourite with the men, some of whom like a good sprinkling of ginger to add zest to the flavour.

METHOD
Cut up the rhubarb and place in a well-buttered pie dish. Trickle the syrup over it. Cream the butter and sugar. Add the eggs, one at a time, having beaten them well. Then fold in the flour and some dry ginger to taste and spread over the fruit. Bake for 40 minutes or so at 375 °F until golden brown.

INGREDIENTS

1 lb rhubarb
4 tablespoons golden syrup
4 oz butter
4 oz sugar
2 eggs
4 oz self-raising flour
ginger to taste

Blackberry Cobbler from Weston-super-Mare

METHOD
Place the washed, juicy blackberries in a greased dish with 2 oz sugar scattered among the fruit. Dot with a little butter. Rub the butter into the flour and stir in the remaining sugar. Knead a little and press gently on the top of the fruit. Bake in a hot oven for 35 minutes. Serve with cream.

INGREDIENTS

1 lb blackberries
4 oz sugar
6 oz plain flour
4 oz butter

WESTON-SUPER-MARE

This lovely photograph from July 1914 is of the fountain at Clarence Park. A small fishing village with little over a hundred people living in it in the early nineteenth century, Weston grew to become the largest town in Somerset after Bath. The Vicar of Wrington, a friend of Hannah More, built a cottage here in 1790. It is now a restaurant. Medical opinion attracted people to

Weston and nearby Uphill, which is situated on a creek used as a port in Roman times. The Royal Hotel was the first to be built in Weston-super-Mare. After the railway arrived in 1841, the population increased dramatically. The Royal Potteries, founded in 1847, supplied Clarence Park with urns, terrace pots, terracotta figures and tiles. Some of Marconi's radio messages in the experimental stage of telephony were broadcast from Brean Down in 1896.

This view of the seafront at Weston-super-Mare dates from the mid-1940s. Attractions, including the museum, the art gallery and the aquarium, were gradually re-opening after the Second World War, but there was always the long, sandy beach. July is the month of carnival.

Apple Charlotte

Named after Queen Charlotte, the wife of George III, this delicious old pudding, still eaten in 'Somersetshire', needs to be made with generous proportions of butter and fruit.

METHOD

Wash, peel and cut up the apples. Cook them gently in a thin layer of water at the bottom of a heavy pan, to which has been added a knob of butter. Cook to a purée, adding sugar to taste. When mixture has cooled, add the egg yolks, well whisked.

INGREDIENTS

1½ lb cooking apples
6 oz unsalted butter
2 egg yolks
½ loaf of real home-baked bread gone stale

Cut the butter into cubes and melt it in a pan until it becomes a yellow oil. Coat the Charlotte tin with some of this. The bread should be free of crusts and cut into neat slices for lining the Charlotte tin – one big slice for the bottom. All slices are dipped in the butter, leaving no gaps between slices. Fill with the apple puree. Make a lid of bread, also dipped in butter. Bake for an hour, first at 400 °F for 20 minutes, then at 375 °F until browned and crisp. It should be served with cream, but we found an egg custard is delicious with this Charlotte.

CLEEVE ABBEY

Early last century, visitors walked 1½ miles from Blue Anchor to Old Cleeve. In a car, one would leave Minehead by Friday Street and Alcombe, and pass Dunster and Carhampton (then the home of the West Somerset Foxhounds), which were glorious with apple orchard blossom in the spring. In the days of this photograph, Cleeve Abbey, a mile from Cleeve, was open on weekdays only, admission 1s. Founded in 1188 by Cistercian monks and dedicated to 'Our Blessed Lady of the Cliffs', the area was originally known as 'the flowery valley'. After the Dissolution of the Monasteries, this building was used in conjunction with a farm for storage, but Mr G. F. Luttrell had it cleaned and cleared, in keeping with its original purpose.

Somerset Pudding

METHOD

Peel, core and cut up the apples and place them in a stewpan with the caster sugar, cinnamon and grated lemon rind. With a small amount of water, stew gently until the apples fall. Crumble the sponge cake, then arrange alternate layers of apple and cake crumbs. Pour the egg custard over this. Whip the egg white stiffly and pile on top. Brown in a slow oven for 5 minutes.

To make the boiled egg custard, beat the eggs and boil the milk. Add it gradually to the strained, beaten eggs. Stir in the sugar. Using a double boiler or standing the custard in a jug in a pan of hot water, stir over gentle heat until the custard is thick and smooth.

INGREDIENTS

2 lb cooking apples
grated rind of a lemon
pinch of cinnamon
6 oz sponge cake
3 oz caster sugar
2 oz icing sugar
white of an egg

For egg custard:
1 pint milk
3 eggs
1 oz sugar

SOMERSET'S CLIFFS

Except at Lynmouth and Porlock, the coast from Minehead to Combe Martin is an almost unbroken cliff 200–300 feet high. Visitors with towing caravans in the 1930s were warned of such dangers as Countisbury, Porlock and Beggar's Roost. 'The land of long, steep climbs' was one guidebook's description.

Early motorists were advised of alternative routes. From Porlock, the north-eastern flank of Exmoor rises 1,000 feet. 'It is impossible to rush this hill, with its sharp bends and gradients from 1 in 8 to 1 in 4,' was how the notorious Porlock Hill was described in the Ward Lock Red Guide. The nervous were advised to climb by the toll road, which zig-zagged about halfway up the hill. Tolls were collected: cars 2s; motorcycles 6d; cycles 3d. The two roads met on Porlock Common.

Stowey Apple Pudding

METHOD
Wash, core, peel and chop the apples. Place them in a
pudding basin lined with crust and cover with a pastry
lid. It was served with sweet cider sauce and it was
unnecessary to add either sugar or water to the pudding.

For the suet crust, mix together the flour, baking powder
and shredded suet, then bind with a little water, enough to
make a firm paste. Use at once. A hundred years ago, some
cooks used beef marrow instead of suet.

To make cider sauce, simmer the cider and sugar
until the volume is much reduced, then add the
unsalted butter. Pour over the apple pudding.

INGREDIENTS

1 lb apples

For the suet crust:
3 oz plain flour
1 teaspoon baking powder
3 oz shredded suet

For the cider sauce:
1 pint cider
4 oz sugar
1 oz unsalted butter

West Country Tart

METHOD
Line a dish with shortcrust pastry. Beat together the
eggs, the slightly warmed syrup, the sugar and the
walnuts. Put this filling in the pastry case and bake in a
moderate oven for half an hour. When cold, it sets. This
was traditionally served with cream. In testing this
recipe, I found that a scatter of shortbread mixture,
just a flurry of the fine crumbs, on top of the filling
was an improvement, the mixture being less likely
to brown around the edges. Definitely for the sweet-
toothed.

INGREDIENTS

6 oz shortcrust pastry
8 oz golden syrup
1 oz brown sugar, pounded
3 oz finely chopped
walnuts

SELWORTHY ALMSHOUSES

Robert Quirke, a mariner working in the years around 1630, founded eleven almshouses 'for and towards the relief, succour and comfort of such distressed poor persons of the Parish of Minehead' (his full statement of intent is held at the Somerset Record Office). Reduced to eight, the almshouses were renovated in the late 1940s and funds, which had dwindled to nothing, were assisted by a sum of £3,000 left by one Thomas Ponsford. The octagonal shaft of an ancient boundary cross stood nearby. This beautiful postcard issued by C. H. Kinnersley of The Square, Minehead, shows the Selworthy almshouses and church. A fairly short but strenuous walk from Minehead via Martlet Road brought the visitor to Selworthy church. Deep, precipitous combes fell away towards the sea on the right, and the road led under Selworthy Beacon (which is at 1,014 feet). Seven thatched cottages and magnificent walnut trees set around the green meant Selworthy could be described as 'the artist's dream' in various guidebooks. Note the tall chimney of a typical Somerset cottage. They were deemed essential for baking bread.

Egg and Apple Tarts from Yeovil

METHOD
Peel and core the apples. Cook until soft, then mash
well. Whisk the eggs well and beat them into the
softened butter and well-mashed apple. Have ready
a sheet of tart tins lined with short-crust pastry. Fill
these with the apple mixture. Put pastry lids on each
tart and cook until nicely browned at 375 °F.

INGREDIENTS

1 lb cooking apples
2 eggs
2 oz sugar
2 oz butter

YEOVIL

Honey-coloured limestone quarried for old buildings in Yeovil sheds a mellow
light over its streets. Montacute House, built from this 'hamstone', is one of the
finest houses in Somerset, and the church of St John the Baptist is known as 'the
lantern of the West Country' because of the light streaming through the high
arches and windows.

Apple Dumplings with Hard Sauce

METHOD
Peel and core the apples. Fill the cavity with caster
sugar, sultanas and clove. Using the pastry recipe for
Bilberry Pie (see page 76), make enough to roll round
each apple. Press the pastry together at the top with a
little water. Place the apple dumplings on a buttered
baking sheet, brushing the tops with yolk of egg.
Bake for half an hour in a hot oven. The dumplings
were brought to table and dusted with sugar. They
reposed in snow-white damask napkins in silver
dishes.

To make the hard sauce, cream the butter and
sugar. Whip the white of an egg stiffly and mix
in (the egg must be at room temperature to avoid
a curdled-looking mixture). Scatter with ground
nutmeg, but sparingly.

INGREDIENTS

6 apples
2 oz caster sugar
2 oz sultanas
1 oz butter
6 cloves
2 egg yolks
sugar for dusting
pastry (see page 76)

For the hard sauce:
4 oz butter
4 oz sugar
egg white
ground nutmeg

Baked Custards

*This was a good standby in old Somerset, especially on
the farms when the farmhands needed feeding. Suet
puddings were another source of energy. Both are
good for keeping warm in wintry weather.*

METHOD
Mix all ingredients together. Pour into a buttered
dish. Bake in a cool oven, at 300 °F.

INGREDIENTS

1 pint milk
4 oz lard
8 oz flour
3 eggs
1 nutmeg, grated
sugar

Cheese Pudding

METHOD
Break the egg. Mix it with milk, breadcrumbs, grated
cheese. If the cheese is very dry, add butter. Put
in a mould and boil for 40 minutes, or bake with
breadcrumbs and a scatter of nutmeg.

INGREDIENTS

1 egg
2 tablespoons milk
1 tablespoon breadcrumbs
¼ lb grated cheese
½ oz butter
grated nutmeg

English Shortbread

*English shortbread made in Somerset is distinguished
by the use of eggs.*

METHOD
Put butter and sugar on a board and cream them
together. Add the eggs well beaten and rub in a little
at a time into the flour, till all is used up. It takes a
good deal of hard kneading. Form the mixture into
two cakes but do not use a rolling pin. Pinch the
edges, prick the centre with a fork, and decorate
with caraway seeds or citron peel. Slip the cakes on
white paper and bake in tins in a moderate oven until
golden brown.

INGREDIENTS

1 lb flour
½ lb moist sugar
½ lb butter
2 eggs
citron peel or caraway seeds

Queen Victoria's Shortbread

The Queen was very fond of these; they became
popular throughout England.

INGREDIENTS

¾ lb flour
½ lb butter
¼ lb sugar

METHOD
Rub in the butter and sugar on a board, then work
in the flour with fingertips. The dough should then
be rolled out to a thickness of an eighth of an inch,
cut into circles, and pricked with a fork. Bake on a
greased tray in a moderate oven for 15 minutes. As an
alternative to raspberry jam, the fruit pulp from raspberry gin could be used with
these shortbreads.

CLEVEDON

Henry Hallam, the historian and friend of Tennyson, had links with Clevedon,
which grew as a seaside resort under the guidance of the Rev. Sir Abraham Elton
until it was termed 'the Hastings of the West'. By 1880, Clevedon had the largest
swimming baths in the West Country. Queen Victoria's Diamond Jubilee was
celebrated by the erection of a clock tower decorated with Elton ware. The local
earthenware was brought in by Sir Edmund Elton and made into souvenirs for
visitors.

Flaky Pastry

Some Somerset cooks declared that lard made the best
pastry. 'Half and half,' they said, cryptically, meaning
equal quantities of of fat and flour. Most important
was adding the right quantity of very cold water
– too much and the pastry is soggy, too little and the
ingredients do not meld and rolling the pastry out flat
is hard to achieve.

INGREDIENTS

8 oz plain flour
8 oz lard
4 tablespoons cold water
pinch of salt

METHOD

Sieve flour and salt into a mixing bowl. Cut half
of the hardened lard into 'chippings' and mix into the flour. Add the water very
gradually to make dough, i.e. pastry. Roll out and add the remainder of the lard in
small quantities all over the rolled-out pastry. Fold over and roll out at least eight
times. Chill the pastry in a fridge and make a lid for your pie crust.

M. SALMET AND HIS MISSING AIRCRAFT

In 1913 and 1914, the French aviator M. Salmet could be found in all sorts of out-
of-the-way places. He gave select passengers short flights, which helped to cover
the overheads and provide an income for the early flyer.

During a visit to Devon and Cornwall in May 1914, Salmet stopped at
Minehead, where he found a wealthy shopkeeper called Halliday, who was keen
to be the first in Minehead to fly with the famous aviator.

Taking off from Minehead, the pair flew along the coast towards Weston-
super-Mare, where, presumably, they planned to land. But they had only travelled
about six miles when, over the seaside town of Watchet, it became necessary to
'ditch' the aircraft in the sea. Both pilot and passenger survived, and the Watchet
lifeboat was launched to rescue them. None of the research I have on this strange
event discloses the fate of the flying machine.

Salmet was driven away in a open-topped Rolls-Royce saloon to Weston and
Watchet returned to near-normal. But what about the aeroplane? Was it broken
so badly that it was abandoned? Was it salvaged? Where is it?

Other Sweets

Zummerzet Fritters

Somerset fritters are different from any other I have come across on my travels. The pancake mixture contains currants and the fritters are cooked in the oven like Yorkshire puddings, but they share the common features of sugar and lemon when cooked. Nothing is better.

METHOD
This recipe goes back to the 1850s and was used for apples, peach and rhubarb fritters: 'To 2 oz of butter, pour on ¼ pint of boiling water. When the butter has melted pour in ¾ pint of cold water. With a pinch of salt and 12 oz of flour, mix in by degrees, beating well until smooth. Stir in the whites of two eggs, beaten stiffly, and use the batter immediately.'

INGREDIENTS

2 oz butter
1 pint water
pinch of salt
12 oz plain flour
whites of 2 eggs
1 lb chopped apple, peach
    or rhubarb

Honey Pudding

Somerset honey was used widely in recipes for puddings and cakes, and in the cooking of ham and chicken. We used Richard Bolton's honey of Mill Fruit Farm, Stogumber, and found it excellent in this recipe.

METHOD

Mix all the ingredients together and mix them well into a stiff consistency. Place in a greased basin, allowing for some expansion. Cover with layers of pleated, buttered paper and steam for 2½ hours.

Page 92 offers a recipe for a suitable sauce.

INGREDIENTS

4 oz brown breadcrumbs made crispy
4 oz flour
4 tablespoons runny honey
4 oz shredded suet
4 oz currants and raisins
1 teaspoon baking powder
a little milk
butter to grease basin

Steamed Fig Pudding

When summer fruits were not available, especially in the months after Christmas, and when all bottled fruit had been used, dried figs, prunes and apricots appeared in puddings. The fruit was washed and soaked overnight.

METHOD
Cream margarine and sugar. Add beaten egg and milk and mix well. Sift the flour and baking powder into the mixture, then add lemon juice and figs. After mixing, pour into a well-greased pudding basin that allows an inch for the mixture to rise. Steam for 2 hours and serve with a sauce – the recipe on page 92 is suitable.

INGREDIENTS

¼ cup margarine
1 cup sugar
1 cup milk
1 egg
2 cups plain flour
4 teaspoons baking powder
1 spoonful fresh lemon juice
2 cups chopped figs

THE WEST SOMERSET RAILWAY COMPANY

On 5 May 1971, the West Somerset Railway Co. was set up and put into action proposals for reopening the line between Minehead and Taunton, formerly the Western Region branch. At 25 miles, it was at that time the longest privately operated railway in Britain. Lord Montagu of Beaulieu opened the stretch between Minehead and Blue Anchor on 28 March 1976 and a service operated four times daily. This has been extended and nowadays Minehead is the western terminus for steam-hauled trains from Bishops Lydeard during the holiday season, while diesel trains carry passengers throughout the year. In this picture, from January 1979, the steaming *Vulcan* heads the Minehead–Stogumber train.

Steamed Marmalade Pudding

METHOD

Grease a 1½ pint pudding basin. Peel and thinly
slice the orange. Line the basin with these slices,
pressing them gently on the grease. Cream the butter
and sugar until fluffy, add the eggs, and fold in the
flour, marmalade and milk. Beat all well together.
Gradually pour this mixture into the basin and
cover with greaseproof paper. Place on an upturned
saucer in a large pan of boiling water and steam for
2 hours, topping up the water as it evaporates.

The pudding can be served with a plain
cornflour sauce. Blend the cornflour and sugar
with 2 tablespoons of milk. Heat the rest of the
milk in a pan until it boils. Pour in the cornflour
and continue to stir until the sauce thickens. Stir
on for a further 2 minutes to ensure that the
cornflour is cooked. Alternatively, an orange
sauce can be made by adding the juice of one
orange and its grated rind to the plain sauce.

INGREDIENTS

3 oz butter
1 orange
3 oz caster sugar
2 beaten free-range eggs
3 oz wholemeal flour
2 tablespoons orange
  marmalade
3 tablespoons milk

For the cornflour sauce:
1 oz patent cornflour
1 oz sugar
¾ pint milk

HARVEST IN SOMERSET

The building that is now the Gables Hotel near Minehead is an example of a
cob-and-thatch dwelling; it has been kept in beautiful state of repair. Examples
of the ancient country craft of corn-dolly making are still to be found round
Somerset – peacocks, birds and cartwheels made from straw adorn the eaves and
rooftops of thatched cottages. The spirit of the corn was thought to survive in the
last sheaf cut from the harvest, which was brought indoors and kept throughout
winter. There was quite a ritual
attached to harvest-cutting. Often
the whole community, led by
the priest (who offered prayers),
would approach the fields. The
first swathe would be cut by the
owner. Until 200 years ago, villages
produced all they needed, with the
blacksmith, wheelwright, saddler,
cobbler and thatcher all backing up
the men who worked in the fields.

Christmas Pudding

METHOD

Put all the ingredients in a large bowl and mix well – first the dry ingredients, then the sherry, brandy and well-beaten eggs. (My grandmother soaked the raisins, currants and sultanas in brandy for a few days before the pudding was made.)

Grease a large pudding basin and put in the mixture. Cover with four layers of greaseproof paper and tie up the basin in a pudding cloth, ready for steaming. The Christmas Pudding requires steaming for 8 hours – 6 hours to cook it and 2 hours extra on Christmas Day itself.

INGREDIENTS

4 oz sultanas
4 oz currants
4 oz raisins
2 oz candied peel
2 oz chopped almonds
4 oz plain flour
4 oz brown breadcrumbs
1 carrot freshly grated
¼ teaspoon cinnamon
3 fl. oz sherry
½ teaspoon mixed spice
3 free range eggs
4 oz Demerara sugar
3 tablespoons brandy
grated rind and juice of 1 lemon
1 apple, cored and grated
4 oz grated suet

HOBBY HORSES

Viking pirates in the ninth century attacked Minehead on a number of occasions until one local crew disguised its ship as a terrifying sea serpent. The raiders fled. Some people think the origin of the Hobby Horse in Minehead relates to this story. Appearing on the eve of May Day and accompanied by drum and accordion, the long and beribboned horse bounds around town for three days, and it could be said that it resembles a Norse longship.

Dunster's hobby horses have a cow's tail. When a ship was wrecked the evening before May Day in 1772, the only item retrieved was a dead cow, 'the tail of which was cut off and used by the toll collectors'.

In some houses the ashen faggot is still burned on Christmas Eve, notably at the Luttrell Arms. The Hobby Horse in Minehead's ancient street is outside a boot-and-shoe shop in 1930.

Gooseberry and Elderflower Fool

My grandmother was a great believer in swishing creamy elderflowers through gooseberry jam in the cooking to improve flavour. She would have liked this recipe.

METHOD
Clean the gooseberries but do not top or tail. Cook in the sugar over a low heat until fruit is soft and mushy. Remove pan from heat and add the elderflowers, stirring gently. Leave for 5 minutes, then discard the flowers. Liquidise the fruit and allow to go cold. Whisk the cream and fold into the gooseberry purée. Leave at the bottom of the fridge until ready to serve.

INGREDIENTS

1 lb gooseberries
4 oz sugar
3 heads elderflower
¼ pint double cream

Prune Puff

METHOD
Whip the egg whites to a stiff froth. Add sugar slowly, still beating. Add the stoned, chopped prunes. Bake in a pudding dish in a moderate oven for 10 minutes. Serve cold with egg custard, made using the egg yolks.

In summer, cream or ice cream accompanied the prune puff.

INGREDIENTS

4 eggs
½ cup powdered sugar
1 large cup cooked prunes

Oat Cakes

METHOD
Mix salt with oatmeal. Melt the butter and put it in a cup. Fill up with the boiling water. Pour this into the oatmeal and beat it very well to get air into the mixture. When it has cooled, knead it into a dough. Sprinkle fine oatmeal onto a baking board and roll out this dough very thinly. Cook on a moderately hot griddle until crisp. The dough can be cut into convenient shapes or rolled out into large ovals.

INGREDIENTS

1 lb medium oatmeal
1 oz fine oatmeal
2 oz butter
½ pint boiling water
½ teaspoon salt

Buttermilk Scones

METHOD

Mix the sugar, baking powder and flour together, then add the beaten eggs and about 1½ cups of buttermilk to make a thin, smooth, lump-free batter. Drop the batter, a little at a time, on a greased, hot griddle and cook for 5 minutes, turning the scones to cook the other side. They are to be eaten fresh with butter.

INGREDIENTS

2 large cups flour
1 tablespoon caster sugar
1½ teaspoons baking powder
2 large eggs
1½ cups buttermilk

Strawberry Ice Cream

This was a rare treat but well worth the effort. The Victorians and Edwardians, some owning ice houses, loved it. We sampled it in Weston-super-Mare.

METHOD

Nowadays we can turn the freezer to 'fast freeze'. Press the button an hour before placing ice cream in the freezer. Pour cream and milk into a chilled bowl and beat both together. Stir in icing sugar and vanilla essence. Stir in the puréed strawberries. Pour into a freezer container and freeze for 45 minutes, then transfer to a chilled bowl and, with a fork, stir and smooth the ice cream. Return to another freezer container and freeze for 2 hours.

INGREDIENTS

1 lb puréed strawberries
1 pint fresh double cream
4 oz sifted icing sugar
2 teaspoons vanilla essence
4 tablespoons fresh milk

THE QUEEN OF ICE CREAM

Of course, the 'queen' of ice cream in those days was Mrs Agnes B. Marshall (1855–1905). Mrs Marshall's four books on ice cream are among the best ever written. She opened a cookery school in London in 1883 and started her own weekly newspaper, *The Table*. She also invented a patent ice cream maker.

Chocolate Fudge

METHOD
Put sugar, cream and chocolate into a pan. Stir and boil until it makes a soft ball when tested in water. Take from the fire. Add the butter. Cool and stir until creamy. Pour onto buttered plates and cut into squares. (NB: One lady I knew used 1 teaspoon of vinegar to help the set.)

INGREDIENTS

3 cups sugar
1 cup cream
2 oz unsweetened
chocolate
1 tablespoon butter

Truffles

METHOD
Cream butter and sugar until light and fluffy. Add cocoa powder, almonds and enough fine crumbs to make a workable paste. Add a small quantity of lemon juice, but be careful not to make the paste soggy. Knead well and roll into a long sausage. Cut into half-inch pieces and roll into balls. Toss into the honey and then roll into the grated chocolate so that every truffle is generously coated.

INGREDIENTS

2 oz caster sugar
2 oz unsalted butter
4 oz ground almonds
2 teaspoons cocoa
finely grated breadcrumbs
from crusts
a little lemon juice
grated plain chocolate
1 tablespoon honey

Nut Butter Toffee

METHOD

Melt the butter in a thick pan over a low heat. Add the sugar, syrup and vinegar and stir well. Bring to the boil and continue stirring until the mixture becomes pale brown. Test a drop in a basin of cold water to see if it hardens. Spread almonds evenly over the base of a shallow bowl and pour the toffee mixture over it. Leave to cool and set.

INGREDIENTS

4 oz butter
8 oz sugar
2 tablespoons vinegar
3 tablespoons golden syrup
4 oz blanched almonds

BRIDGWATER

Below is a postcard of St Mary's church in Bridgwater. There has been a church on this site since at least the start of the twelfth century. The present building has been radically altered many times, and there are presently plans to turn its membership into an 'Eco-Congregation'. The four-day St Matthew's Fair in September and the Guy Fawkes Carnival in November are important.

Stuffed Dates

METHOD

These dates are stuffed with the honey nut toffee. Use good-quality, boxed dates. Remove stones from dates. Fill the holes with the honey nut toffee.

To make honey nut toffee, boil the honey in a strong saucepan for 12 minutes. Have a greased tin handy, covered with the chopped nuts. Pour honey onto the nuts. When cold, it can be broken into lumps and wrapped as individual pieces, using screws of greaseproof paper.

INGREDIENTS

1 box dates

For the honey nut toffee
½ lb honey
¼ lb chopped nuts

HONEY

The use of honey in Somerset recipes was more marked than in many other regions I have visited. When he visited Britain, Pliny the Elder wrote, 'These islanders consume great quantities of honey brew.' He meant mead. He believed it was good for a person's health and long life and there are reports that he met 124 beekeepers, all of whom were over a hundred years old. In her diary, a seventeenth-century farmer's wife regretted that, in getting the honey, she and her husband had to kill the bees the only way they knew: '… dig a hole in the ground for each skeppe where we put a sulfur paper, set alight and put the skeppe

of bees on the topp … we do want the honey, using a gret lot in the hous'. Her favourite dish was 'honey cake and rollies', but in all areas it was used in many culinary pursuits. 'Telling' the bees is an old custom, especially when the head of the house dies. This is so that the bees will not forsake the bereaved.

Orange Medley

METHOD
Blend all into a purée. Chill and serve.

INGREDIENTS

1 tablespoon natural yoghurt
½ pint freshly squeezed orange juice
1 banana
1 free-range egg

BLAGDON

W. D. & H. O. Tobacco Company of Bristol had Coombe Lodge, situated near Blagdon, pulled down. A mock-Tudor mansion was built on the site in the 1930s. Not far away is Burrington, where the famous 'Rock of Ages', which inspired the well-known hymn of that name, is situated.

At Blagdon, Yeo Valley Organic's probiotic yoghurt is made. It is delicious alone or with pies, puddings and fruit. Yeo Valley Organic is family-owned and proud of its roots in Somerset.

Ciders, Wines, Pickles, Jams, Etc.

Somerset Farm Cider

METHOD
Wash apples and cut up roughly. Pour the boiling water over them. Allow to stand for two weeks. Strain and add 1 lb Demerara sugar to each quart of liquor.

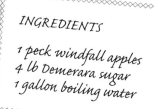

INGREDIENTS

1 peck windfall apples
4 lb Demerara sugar
1 gallon boiling water

WASSAILING THE APPLE TREES

On Twelfth Night, the farmers of Somerset wassailed their apple trees, which meant standing around in a circle and singing to encourage a good apple crop for puddings, pies and cider. After cider was poured onto the roots of the apple trees, wassailing could commence: 'Here's to the old apple tree! Hats full, caps full, bushel sacks full!' In Carhampton, the custom is still part of the calendar – wassailing takes place on 17 January each year.

Rough Somerset Cider

This is an untested recipe, but I have been warned of its potency. In the past, abuse of cider led to many a fight among labourers and seamen, but the number of apple recipes in this book alone shows how fond the West Country people are of the cause of Adam and Eve's downfall.

METHOD
Place the washed apples in a wooden tub and crush them. Pour the boiling water over them, cover with a scalded cloth and leave for a fortnight. Mash up the apples daily.

'After the fortnight, strain off the liquor and put in the bruised ginger root and half a pound of sugar to every pint of cider. Add a little extra boiling water. Stir well and put in the lemon juice and the halved lemon cases. Leave for another fortnight.

Skim off any scum. Remove the lemon halves and ginger root and bottle lightly for three days, after which the tops can be firmly fixed and the cider left for two months before drinking.'

INGREDIENTS

8 lb apples
8 lb sugar
4 lemons
1 fair-sized piece of ginger root
2 gallons boiling water

THE GEORGE INN, NORTON ST PHILIP

This old postcard shows the tap room of the George Inn and bears the caption, 'The cellars of this old inn were used as dungeons for the prisoners of war after the skirmish between the Royalists and Monmouth's troops shortly before the Battle of Sedgemoor.' On the main route towards Bath, this ancient inn was very busy during a three-day fair held since 1255, when linen and woollen cloth were sold. Built of local brown stone with a jettied timber frame, the George, one of the most famous buildings in Somerset, was the focal point and is referred to in a document from 1638. The diarist Pepys dined here 'very well'. In the Duke of Monmouth's day there was stabling for ninety horses and the crested mail coach, shown on another page, would certainly clatter up here, announcing its arrival from a distance by the long post horn.

The George Inn claims to be the oldest licensed house in England. It is steeped in history – it was where the Duke of Monmouth stayed the night before the Battle of Sedgemoor. He was fired at by a Somerset man, who hoped to win the £1,000 reward on the Duke's head.

Nettle Beer

METHOD

Boil the nettle tops with the ginger, lemon rinds and water. Simmer for ¾ of an hour. Strain the liquid onto the lemon juice, cream of tartar and sugar. Sprinkle the yeast on top. Allow it to work and when working has ceased, put into large stone jars. Top up as necessary. Cork and leave for 3 months, then put into sterilised bottles.

INGREDIENTS

1½ lb young, well-washed nettles
1½ oz ginger
2 lemons
1 lb Demerara sugar
1 oz cream of tartar
1 tablespoon dried yeast

RECREATION IN MINEHEAD

Minehead and district, with so much moor, woodland and cliff to offer, has long been popular for walking. In the 1890s, high wagonettes afforded splendid views over the countryside. Accommodation in cottages and farmhouses was plentiful, and when the cycling craze arrived in the 1890s, offers of cream teas and herb beer or nettle drink were well patronised at wayside cottages. The original Minehead Harriers, a pack of hounds, were kennelled locally and hunted hares over the extensive moorlands. The opening meet of the Minehead Harriers was at East Lynch Farm. By the first quarter of the twentieth century, a modern highway covered the once-wild road across Exmoor, which was haunted by the Doones and highwayman Tom Faggus. As for railway routes, Minehead, 168 miles from London Paddington, was served by fast expresses, which covered the distance in 4 hours.

Dandelion Wine

METHOD
To make 2 gallons, pour 4 quarts of boiling water over 5 quarts of washed dandelion flowers and leave to stand. A day later, boil 4 quarts of water with 8 lb of sugar and the rind. Strain the liquor off the flowers and place all together in a large crock. Mix the yeast with some of the warm (not hot) liquor, then add it to the crock. Put it into large stone jars and allow it to work for 3 weeks, filling up the jars with boiled water for the first 2 weeks. Cork and leave for 6 months, then put into small, sterilised bottles, but do not disturb the sediment.

INGREDIENTS

2 gallons water
5 quarts washed
   dandelion flowers
8 lb sugar
rind of 1 lemon and
   2 oranges
1 oz yeast

THE HUNGERFORDS

Farleigh Hungerford Castle and the estate village of Kilmersdon are Somerset gems set close to the border with Wiltshire. With ice cream and herb beer in mind, a cool inn to enjoy on a hot summer's day is the Joliffe Arms. Architect James Wyatt and Thomas A. Joliffe MP were associated with Ammerdown House, where the fields of golden yellow dandelions are perfect for making wine.

Although it is 300 years since a member of the Hungerford family ruled this part of Somerset, the Joliffe family nevertheless carved, in three languages, the name on a 150-foot-high stone column, which is topped with a lantern.

The Hungerfords have a 'living' coat of arms. Their heraldic device consists of a sheaf of wheat and two crossed sickles, and it is yearly displayed fresh in St Leonard's church.

Dandelion and Ginger Wine

The end of April and the beginning of May is the time to make this lovely brew. All the way from Somerset to Devon, golden, glowing dandelions smiled down the winding lanes and across the fields.

METHOD
The flowers should be covered with the boiling water, left for three days and stirred frequently. The liquid should then be strained and the ginger, orange and lemon rinds added. Bring to the boil and simmer the solution for 35 minutes.

Now squeeze the juices from the lemon and orange and add immediately to the raisins and sugar and yeast and leave in a warm place to ferment for eight days. Strain the wine into a 1 gallon jar. As the wine clears, it can be bottled. Keep till Christmas.

INGREDIENTS

1 lb dandelion flower heads
1 gallon boiling water
1 lemon
1 oz ground ginger
8 oz raisins
1 orange
5 lb sugar
2 oz yeast

Elderberry Wine

METHOD

The berries should be black and ripe (watch the starlings – they know). Strip from the stalks and measure. Place in pan and pour water over them, stirring and pressing well. Each day for five days continue to stir and press, then press out as much juice as possible through a hair sieve. Measure the juice, putting 2 gallons into a preserving pan with the sugar and spices. Gently boil all for three-quarters of an hour, then strain into a porcelain dish, floating on the toast spread with yeast. Cover with a cloth and leave for four days. After skimming, place in a cask and make sure the bung is left loose until hissing ceases. Only then should it be bunged tightly. Leave for four months before bottling.

INGREDIENTS

5 lb elderberries
2 gallons water
6 lb Demerara sugar
½ oz allspice
4 oz ground ginger
2 tablespoons yeast
a piece of toast

ENTERTAINMENT IN MINEHEAD

In the early 1900s, a favourite meeting place for locals and visitors was the Plume of Feathers hotel. Entertainment was at the Queen's Theatre, the Strand. Gladys Cooper, one of the most famous beauties of her day, appeared here after the First World War, as did ballerina Anna Pavlova. In those days it was known as Queen's Hall. The Queen's could accommodate 850 people. There were daily orchestral concerts on the Promenade in summer and entertainers such as the Pierrots would perform in the Jubilee Gardens, and in the Arcadia if it was wet. From June to September at the Regal Cinema and the Gaiety Theatre near the railway station, concert parties took place. The Regal Cinema also had a ballroom. On the beach, visitors enjoyed pony races and aquatic sports, plus the usual paddling and sandcastle-making.

Plum Wine

Dark, ripe plums give this drink the 'port' look.

METHOD
Remove stalks from plums and wipe with a cloth.
Place in an earthenware bowl or ceramic dish along
with the ginger, cinnamon and cloves. Cover with
a gallon of boiling water and leave for a fortnight,
stirring night and morning. Then add the sugar,
stirring well until all has completely dissolved.
Strain into a cask and in six months' time the plum
wine will be ready to bottle.

INGREDIENTS

4 lb plums
1 gallon water
3 lb granulated sugar
1 oz root ginger
a stick of cinnamon
15 cloves

Old English Mead

METHOD
Dissolve honey in water, add hops, and simmer
for an hour. When the honey liquid has cooled
to lukewarm, add the yeast. Cover and leave
for four days, then strain into jars. During
fermentation, keep the jars topped up. Cork
tightly when working has ceased and do not
drink for a year.

INGREDIENTS

1½ lb honey
1 gallon water
½ lb dried hops
1 oz yeast

MALMSMEAD

Malmsmead village and bridge, shown in this old photograph of 1920, was
popular because it boasted the farm from *Lorna Doone*, which is on the right
of the inn, partly hidden by trees. I still have the visiting card issued by A. D.
French, the proprietor who was receiving visitors in the 1920s: 'Day parties
supplied with luncheons, teas, minerals … saddled ponies to the Doone Valley for
hire … Furnished Apartments Malmsmead, Lorna Doone Farm, Brendon.' At
Malmsmead, a mile from Dare, Badgworthy Water joins the River Lyn – which
John Ridd, hero of *Lorna Doone*, described as 'a good stream, as full of fish as of
pebbles'. Cloud Farm Tea Garden, situated about a mile from Malmsmead, was
also visited.

Allerford Raspberry Gin

METHOD
Wash raspberries and place in glass sweet jar or
any other suitable container (a plastic sweet jar will
suffice). Pour on the gin. Tightly screw on the cap. Give
jar a good shake every day. Keep in a warm place for
five days. After five days, boil the water. Stir in sugar
until it has dissolved. When cool, pour into jar. Keep
jar in a warm, dark place for three months. Sieve
liquid and bottle. Save pulp as filling for a Victoria
Sandwich. Can be drunk as soon as it has been bottled.

INGREDIENTS

2 lb fresh raspberries
1 pint cheap gin
2 pints water
1 lb sugar

ALLERFORD

Another typical Somerset village close to Minehead, pictured in 1910. In the
centre are the lovely old packhorse bridge and the old cottages. All around
Bossington, Allerford and Selworthy, picturesque woods – all open to the public
– clothed the hillsides. These were so honeycombed with tracks – offering 30
miles of walking – it was possible to get lost. Agnes Fountain, at the back of
Allerford village, is named after a daughter of Sir Thomas Acland, who is himself
commemorated by the huge wooden cross put up in 1898 on the far side of the
bridge.

Fruit Punch

METHOD
Strain the juice from the oranges and lemons
and mix it with the pineapple and cider. Boil
the sugar with half a pint of hot water for 10
minutes. Add the fresh raspberries and simmer
for 5 minutes, then strain off the syrup. Mix
it with the fruit juices and, when cold, the
spring water. The punch can be hot or, in a hot
summer, iced.

INGREDIENTS

4 oranges
3 lemons
½ lb fresh raspberries
6 oz caster sugar
1 teacup crushed fresh
    pineapple
1 pint spring water
½ pint cider

Dunkery Lemonade

INGREDIENTS

rind of 4 lemons cut fine
juice of 6 lemons
4 lb sugar
1 oz citric acid
3 pints water

METHOD
Mix together and pour on the water, boiling. In
use, it will dilute.

DUNKERY BEACON

About four miles west of
Minehead, by ascending
Chapel Steep, just beyond
Luccombe, the summit of
Dunkery Beacon can be
reached. Visitors are told of
the ancient beacon hearths.
John Fry in *Lorna Doone*
calls Dunkery Beacon 'the
highest place on Hexmoor'

(it is 1,707 feet). Here the Doones lit their beacon fires in time of danger. Two
nearby hills, Robin How and Jinny How, also had beacon hearths. Dunkery
Beacon is crowned by a cairn and the remains of the hearths, upon which the
beacons were piled. These old beacon fires could spread the warning of attack from
Plymouth to the Malvern Hills, for both are visible from Dunkery. In September
1935, a ceremony was held when the National Trust received the gift of the largest
land area ever offered, i.e. Dunkery Beacon and 9,000 acres of surrounding
moorland. At that time, there were daily coach trips over Dunkery in the summers.
The photograph by Vowles (above) dates from early in the last century.

The second view is of Dunkery Beacon from Porlock Hill and gives a good
impression of space and light. When the estate was sold, a report by the National
Trust stated, 'To be the owner of Dunkery is no small thing for from its summit
there is a prospect unsurpassed in the kingdom and no fewer than 15 counties
with an horizon calculated at 500 miles.' I recall the view from Dunkery as
magnificent and remember finding wild cherries growing in the hedges at the
foot of the Beacon.

Kali

METHOD

Add the essence to the sugar, then the other powders (all the powders should be dry). Stir and pass twice through a hair sieve, so that they are well mixed. Kali must be kept in tightly corked bottles and only a dry spoon inserted. A large teaspoon dissolved in a two-thirds-full tumbler of water makes a refreshing, if acidic, drink, which was much appreciated eighty years ago, along with nettle beer, herb beer, broom wine and ginger ale – all of which could be produced cheaply.

INGREDIENTS

½ lb ground white sugar
¼ lb bicarbonate of soda
¾ lb tartaric acid
40 drops of lemon essence

Blackberry Vinegar

Midland and northern regions tend to favour raspberry vinegar, but the West Country, so prolific in blackberries, has used them for their sore throat remedy for over a hundred years.

INGREDIENTS

4 lb blackberries
2 pints vinegar
1 lb sugar to each pint of juice produced

METHOD

Wash and crush the blackberries, then pour the vinegar over, or enough to cover. Leave them covered for a whole day, then boil with the sugar for 25 minutes. It should thicken a little. Bottle when cold. A tablespoonful in a glass of hot water makes a delicious drink, regardless of colds.

Coleslaw

This recipe for Coleslaw found its way to Somerset from Canada. It should be made a day previous to requirements and stored in the refrigerator to be used up completely while fresh.

METHOD
After mixing the chopped vegetables together in a bowl, add the yoghurt, salad cream and milk. Mix very well and very gradually stir in the white vinegar and a squeeze of lemon juice.

INGREDIENTS

1 finely chopped cabbage
1 finely chopped onion
1 medium-sized carrot, grated
small carton plain yoghurt
½ small bottle salad cream
1 tablespoon milk
1 dessertspoon white vinegar
lemon juice

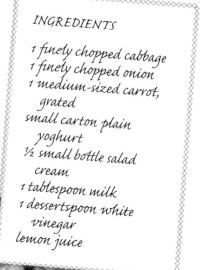

Salad Dressing

METHOD

This very simple salad dressing must always be made freshly. Mix together the vinegar, dry mustard, lemon juice and sugar. Finally add the cream, which should be beaten in very slowly.

INGREDIENTS

1 teaspoon distilled vinegar
1 teaspoon dry mustard
a little lemon juice
a little sugar
1 tablespoon cream

BLENHEIM GARDENS, MINEHEAD

Mature trees in the well-established park in 1963. Enclosed by the triangle of roads – North Road, Blenheim Road and the Avenue – the Blenheim Gardens were easily reached from the Esplanade and Hotel Metropole. As traffic increased in volume and the town became busier, the Blenheim Gardens have been more and more appreciated. The park can be enjoyed all year round as a meeting place.

Irnham Recreation Ground, flanked by Queens Road and Tregonwell Road, had a pavilion. On its fourth boundary, Alexandra Road, were the tennis courts.

Mayonnaise

For really good mayonnaise, the distinctive flavour of tarragon vinegar is essential.

METHOD
The ingredients should be blended together in a bowl and beaten with a fork until smooth. Work on half the quantities first, and when these are smoothly blended bring in the other half. Keep in a cool place and always shake well before use.

   Herbs can be added to this dressing. Alternatively, beat in 2 oz of cream cheese with half of a small minced onion. Another variant is a crushed clove of garlic. Peel the clove (one only), crush it well in a mortar, and mix it thoroughly into the dressing.

INGREDIENTS

2 tablespoons of tarragon vinegar
4 tablespoons olive oil (or corn oil)
½ teaspoon dry mustard
½ teaspoon sugar
a dash of freshly ground sea salt
a dash of peppercorns

Roux

METHOD

Roux is melted butter combined with an equal amount of flour and is used as a basis for the thickening of soups, gravies and sauces. Use a low heat and mingle the flour and butter slowly until smooth.

INGREDIENTS

2 oz flour
2 oz butter

Cheese Sauce for Poached Fish

METHOD
Heat the butter and stir in the flour. Allow it to cook for 2 minutes, then gradually add the stock and milk, stirring all the time to ensure smoothness. Add the cheese and continue the stirring. Put in a very little seasoning and cook on for 6 minutes to ensure flour is cooked; otherwise, it will not taste nice.

INGREDIENTS

½ pint fish stock
½ pint milk
2 oz butter
2 oz flour
seasoning
4 tablespoons grated Cheddar cheese

CLOVELLY

Two paddle steamers are pictured off Clovelly in around 1900. The sixteenth-century harbour provides a shelter for its fishing boats. The photograph was taken from high up, in an area so steep that cottages and shops seem to stand on top of one another. The Clovelly Dykes, Iron Age earthworks covering 20 acres, were interesting to visitors, but especially so was the steep, cobbled, stepped street leading to this tiny harbour. It was once the bed of a rushing stream that emptied into the sea.

The stone-built quay at Clovelly was made by George Cary, whose family had owned the manor since the reign of Richard I. A charge of fourpence was made in the 1930s for pedestrians to traverse the beautifully wooded Hobby Drive; cycles and donkeys paid sixpence and carriages 1s 6d. In those days, the steep, cobbled street of Clovelly was busy with pannier-laden donkeys, some carrying passengers 'whose weight is under seven stone' according to the Donkey Charter. Giant fuchsias covered the fronts of some cottages, and the street, culminating in wide steps, was crowded with visitors. This lovely photograph dates from the 1890s and shows two Bideford fishing boats.

Pickled Plums

Very good with Christmas meats.

METHOD
Put the fruit or fruit pulp in with the sugar. Add the spices and vinegar and cook until tender. Drain well and put into jars. Boil the syrup for a quarter of an hour and strain into the jars. On the next day, pour off the syrup, re-boil, and pour over the fruit again. Allow to go cold, cover it, and store for three months. If pickled in September, the plums will be ready for use on the Christmas dinner table.

INGREDIENTS

3 lb plums or plum pulp
1 teaspoon allspice
2 lb sugar
1 teaspoon ginger
4 pints vinegar
1 teaspoon ground cloves

GLASTONBURY

After sampling strawberries and Cheddar Cheese (albeit not on the same plate), a visitor's next priority would be to take a motor charabanc tour to Glastonbury and Cheddar Gorge. In 1934 an American visitor wrote, 'Worth coming 7,000 miles to see.' He was referring to Cox's Cave, Cheddar, and no doubt he also went on to Glastonbury to investigate the legend of the Holy Thorn, which was supposedly planted by Joseph of Arimathea and flowers only at Christmas.

The whole plain of Glastonbury was once the seabed. The sea once covered much of the land between the Quantocks and the Mendip Hills. This Raphael Tuck postcard from the 1900s shows the Abbot's Kitchen at Glastonbury Abbey, a massive stone structure with an octagonal interior and four huge fireplaces. In the days of this photograph it was used as a museum for storing some of the relics turned up in excavations. St Mary's Chapel, the Pilgrims' Inn (which became the George Hotel), and Glastonbury Tor (in the Vale of Avalon with its possible associations with King Arthur) all have associated traditions that appeal to the imagination.

From the low-lying Somerset Levels there is a fine view of Glastonbury Tor. It is thought that Cadbury Castle could have been the site of Camelot. Most beautiful is an avenue of beech trees leading to an Elizabethan mansion, Cadbury Court.

Parsley Honey

Parsley honey was recommended for the nerves.

METHOD
Place freshly picked, washed parsley in a pan so that
it is half full. Boil for half an hour with the water and
the rind. Strain and to every pint of juice produced,
add the juice of 2 lemons and 1 lb of sugar. Boil
quickly until it thickens into a syrup. Pot as you do
jam. The parsley honey was eaten as a sweetmeat
on bread and butter or with cold meats, like mint
jelly.

INGREDIENTS

1 bunch fresh parsley
rind of 1 lemon
juice of 2 lemons
¼ pint soft water
1 lb sugar

CARVING AND TRACKLEMENTS

Old-fashioned carving terms come to mind in dealing with poultry and game,
some Victorians excelling at the florid expression: spoiling a hen; winging a
partridge; embracing a mallard; thighing a woodcock. The eighteenth-century
accompaniments to meat dishes were known as tracklements and might
consist of melon, orange, peaches, redcurrant or wild raspberry stuffing. Today's
universally accepted condiment for duck seems to be orange sauce, but real
fruit jellies containing scant sweetening, e.g. redcurrant, rowan or rose hip, are
excellent, counteracting any fattiness that may be present.

Chutney

METHOD
The garlic, raisins and apples (or gooseberries) are
boiled in the vinegar until soft, then they are put
through a sieve. The other ingredients are to be
added and boiled up.

INGREDIENTS

2 lb brown sugar
1 lb raisins
2 oz ground ginger
2 oz mustard
¼ oz cayenne pepper
¼ lb garlic
¼ lb salt
2 lb sour apples or
 gooseberries
3 pints malt vinegar

Damson Pickle

METHOD
Stone the fruit (quite the hardest part) and pour the cider vinegar over the damsons. Leave them for 14 hours, then on the next day strain off the juice, boil it up, and pour once more over the fruit. Repeat this process, add sugar, then boil all up together for half an hour. Remove the cloves in muslin and put the pickled damsons in clean, warm jars.

INGREDIENTS

3 lb damsons
2 lb sugar
1 teaspoon cloves encased in muslin
¾ pint cider vinegar

Sweet Pickle

This is a useful way to use windfall apples, which in some years were so plentiful in Somerset that passers-by were invited to take whatever they wanted. The golden rule is to use delicately flavoured honeys with light ingredients and the stronger honeys with strong-flavoured ingredients.

METHOD
Mix honey, vinegar, cinnamon and cloves together and boil. Cook a quarter of the apples in this syrup. When cooked, carefully remove the apples, then cook the rest in the same way. Remove cloves from syrup. Store the apples in sterilised jars, pouring the syrup equally over them. Seal and label.

INGREDIENTS

6 cloves
1 cup vinegar
2 cups Somerset clover
3 lb washed, quartered apples
½ cup acacia honey
2 pinches cinnamon

Apricot Sauce

'A sauce to improve any pudding,' said one guest.

METHOD
Put ten stoned, ripe apricots through a sieve and purée. Put this pulp into a jam pan and dilute with the syrup sauce. Bring to the boil, adding a tot of Kirsch or cherry brandy liqueur. When the sauce coats the back of a spoon, it is ready.

INGREDIENTS

10 stoned, ripe apricots
½ pint light syrup sauce
a tot of Kirsch

MINEHEAD'S SEAFRONT

Another period piece from 1925 shows Minehead's Strand Promenade and
Bathing Beach. Here are more vintage cars, and the mile-long seafront framing
a beach with a huge expanse of sand can be well appreciated from this particular
postcard. The tide ebbs for over half a mile. Bathing is safe at high water in the
shelter of the harbour, but strong tidal currents are a feature of the outer stretches
of the bay. Obviously this is a very pleasant, quiet seaside resort, and 'next door'
lies the attractions of another – Blue Anchor Bay. A mile or so beyond that,
the interesting port of Watchet can be visited. In the winter of 1900, a fierce
storm, which coincided with an unusually high tide, destroyed the harbour. It
was rebuilt. Old, wooden piers were once used for loading iron ore mined in
the Brendon Hills for shipping to South Wales. Watchet is the ancient port
where Samuel Taylor Coleridge was regaled with seafaring tales from old sailors,
inspiring his well-known poem 'The Rime of the Ancient Mariner'.

Cider Sauce

This is a good old Somerset sauce for steamed puddings such as Honey Pudding (see page 90).

METHOD
Grate the rind from the lemons, then squeeze out the juice. Place into a saucepan with sugar, cider and water. Mix well and simmer for an hour until the mixture becomes syrupy.

INGREDIENTS

2 lemons
¼ pint cider
¼ pint water
8 oz sugar

Plum Syrup for Fruit Salads

METHOD
Bring the plums and sugar to the boil, then simmer for 20 minutes. Pour through a sieve and drain. Measure the syrup and to each quart add 1 teaspoon of brandy. Bottle and cork well. The plum pulp can be made into pickled plums (see below).

INGREDIENTS

7 lb plums
7 lb sugar
1 teaspoon brandy to every quart of syrup

Almond Custard

This old recipe is typical of a score of custards with which the Victorians were familiar, but which have died out. It is well worth the expense and extra trouble if you want to treat your palate.

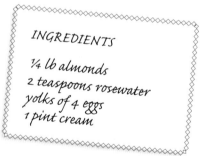

INGREDIENTS

¼ lb almonds
2 teaspoons rosewater
yolks of 4 eggs
1 pint cream

METHOD
The sweet almonds should be pounded in a mortar (nowadays ready-ground almonds can be found in supermarkets). Stir in the rosewater, then the yolks of eggs and finally the cream. Instruction continues: 'Put this over a slow fire and keep it constantly stirred till it has reached its proper thickness. Pour into cups.' The constant stirring is important and a double saucepan is excellent for the job.

This recipe is taken from the sixth edition of an old cookery book, *Everyday Dishes*, sponsored by Lyle's Golden Syrup c. 1900.

Syllabub

Somerset, a county of rich pastures, has for centuries enjoyed syllabub. To produce the creamy froth, the farmer's wife milked straight from the cow into the bowl. Usually the breed was Red Poll, famed for its rich milk, which was excellent for making cream. In Elizabethan days, 'sack', a mead, was added, but later practice favoured wine, sherry or brandy.

INGREDIENTS

3 oz caster sugar
2 tablespoons brandy
2 tablespoons sherry
10 oz double cream
juice and grated rind of
1 lemon

METHOD

For at least 3 hours soak the lemon rind in the lemon juice. Add sugar, brandy and sherry, then add all this gradually to the thick cream, mixing thoroughly. Traditionally this was served with sponge fingers or almond macaroons.

THE OLD PRIORY, MINEHEAD

This 1930s postcard shows the doorway and mounting steps of Old Priory, described in early guides as the oldest building in Lower Town, Minehead. By the 1950s, it was used as a tearoom. It was also referred to as the Manor Office, where manor rates in connection with the Dunster Estate were paid. The ancient door, the diamond-paned oak windows, and the steps for mounting horses are all interesting. There is no evidence that the building was used for religious gatherings.

4673. Doorway & Mounting Steps, Old Priory, Minehead.

Halsway Strawberry Jam

Four-year-old Inona (below right, with the strawberry jam face) can recommend this recipe, which is deliciously different from the usual. It includes a quarter-pound of Somerset honey.

INGREDIENTS

2 lb strawberries (or raspberries)
3 lb sugar
¼ lb Somerset honey
juice of 1 large lemon

METHOD

Wash and mash the fruit and put into the preserving pan, then add the sugar. Stir well. Add honey and blend using a wooden spoon. Sustain a rolling boil for 5 minutes after adding the lemon juice. Continue stirring for a few minutes more, then pour into hot, sterilised jars and cover while hot.

Raspberry Jam

METHOD

Put raspberries in a heavy preserving pan over a gentle heat. Mash with a wooden spoon until juices run. The warmed sugar should then be added and, once dissolved, brought quickly to the boil. Allow 3 minutes and no more. Pour into jars and seal. Used in a winter pudding with a light sponge, it brings summer into the room. It is the best filling for Victoria Sponge Cake.

INGREDIENTS

4 lbs raspberries
5 lbs preserving sugar

Bramble Jelly

Many pounds of blackberries were collected during the Second World War, but long before this the fruit was gathered from copses and roadside hedges that had never been sprayed with chemicals. Nowadays watch out for this – do not pick berries from roadsides where fumes may have polluted the fruit with lead. Gather the ripe berries on a dry day in an enamel can.

INGREDIENTS

6 lb ripe blackberries, stalks removed
3 lb cooking apples
¾ lb preserving or jam sugar to every pint of juice

METHOD
Wipe apples after rinsing and cut into quarters, but do not peel or core them. Put in jam pan and cover with water. Boil and simmer until apples are tender. Strain off the juice in a hair sieve. Run cold water over the blackberries. Put in the pan and simmer until they are soft. The water will turn dark red. Drain off this juice through the hair sieve and mix the two fruits together. Put the liquid into the preserving pan using ¾ lb sugar to every pint of juice and boil quickly until it sets (this takes about half an hour). Turn into warmed jars and seal.

PADDLE STEAMERS IN THE BRISTOL CHANNEL

Owned by the Barry & Bristol Channel Steamship Co., SS *Gwalia*, or 'Devonia', was in 1905 one of the many paddle steamers to be seen near Minehead. Most unusually, there is no carefree reference to sunny weather or holidays in the message written on the back of this postcard, only stark facts highlighting the hazards of shipping: 'Rohilla Morn ex-P&O Rohilla is reported sunk and a total loss off Ijina after being discharged from transport duties.' The information, dated 11 July 1905, was intended for a Lancashire mill and ship owner.

Seville Orange Marmalade

METHOD
Scrub the fruit to ensure cleanliness. Cut each into
two and squeeze out juices. Place these shells of fruit
into a large earthenware bowl and cover with the
water. Soak for at least a day, with a small muslin
bag of the fruit pips suspended in the water. Next,
simmer these skins for 2 hours in the preserving
pan. Rough cut or shred finely the cooled skins
as desired. Return the muslin bag of pips to the
pan and boil all up again with the fruit juices and the sugar,
dissolving the latter gradually. The pips in the muslin bag are important as they
add flavour and aid the set. After the sugar and juice have been added it should be
necessary to boil rapidly for only 15 minutes. Test that it has set then put it in warm,
clean jars and seal at once.

INGREDIENTS

6 Seville oranges
2 lemons
6 lb preserving sugar
4 pints water

Blackberry Curd

This was a completely new and delicious sweetmeat
to me. The recipe makes 6 lbs of curd.

METHOD
Simmer the peeled and cored apples and the blackberries in sufficient water to cover them. When the
fruit is soft, pour through a sieve into a double boiler.

INGREDIENTS

2 lb blackberries
¾ lb apples
8 oz butter
6 eggs
juice of 2 lemons
2 ½ lb lump sugar

Add the lemon juice, cut-up butter
and sugar. When all has dissolved,
add the strained, well-beaten eggs
and cook until mixture thickens,
stirring all the time. When the
mixture coats the back of the
wooden spoon, it is ready. Pour
into warm, sterilised jars and seal,
but do not expect to store it as
long as jam.

Rosemary Syrup

Flowers, fruits and herbs used in cooking and drink-making were gathered when the dew had dried off them and before the sun became too hot. Fruit should be just ripe. This cough remedy is very old, coming from a fragment of manuscript dated 1860.

INGREDIENTS

2 pints water
a handful of rosemary
2 lb sugar

METHOD
Pour the boiling water onto the chopped rosemary
and leave it to stand overnight. Strain the liquid next day
and to each pint of liquid add 1 lb of sugar. Boil until syrupy and allow to cool, when
it may be bottled. A sore-throat remedy.

OLD COUNTRY REMEDIES

◊ To relieve a bruise take one handful of chamomile flowers or elder flowers, half
a pint of vinegar and a quarter of a pint of brandy. Boil the flowers in a pint
of water. Strain into jug. Add vinegar and brandy. To be applied as hot as the
sufferer can bear.

◊ A potato poultice was thought to give relief from sunburn. It was made from
grated raw potato spread between gauze.

◊ To soothe unbroken chilblains, boil 9 oz of celery stalks in 2 pints of water.
When cool, dip the hands or feet in the pitcher.

◊ Fig leaves boiled with honey were a remedy for coughs and colds.

◊ To remove a wart, rub it with radish juice twice a day.

◊ A few leaves of sage or a pinch of aniseed in a cup of boiling water will relieve
indigestion.

◊ To cure insomnia, use a pillow filled with hops.

◊ To relieve pleurisy, apply leeks cooked in a cabbage leaf.

◊ Rosemary leaves soaked in wine were used to soothe bee or wasp stings.

◊ Long ago there was a belief that headaches could be charmed away by
touching a rope that had been used for a public hanging.

About the Author

Catherine Rothwell is a local history specialist and a Fellow of the Library Association. She has won four literary awards, most recently the Titus Wilson Award in the Lake District Book of the Year Competition 2006, for *Along the River Kent*. As a historian, one of her abiding interests has been old cooking methods and implements. She fed a family of six for fifty years and has amassed a huge collection of recipes – including many old, handwritten ones that have been part of her family life for decades. She is an occasional broadcaster on television and radio, and this is her eighty-first book.